Make It Plant-Based!
Southern

Make It Plant-Based! Southern

Southern

50+ RECIPES FOR VEGAN BISCUITS, CASSEROLES, SOUPS, STEWS, AND SWEETS

Mehreen Karim

Photographs by Emma Fishman

WORKMAN PUBLISHING · NEW YORK

Workman
Workman Publishing
Hachette Book Group, Inc.
1290 Avenue of the Americas
New York, NY 10104
workman.com

Workman is an imprint of Workman Publishing, a division of Hachette Book Group, Inc. The Workman name and logo are registered trademarks of Hachette Book Group, Inc.

Design by Suet Chong
Cover illustration by str33t cat/Shutterstock, Inc.

The publisher is not responsible for websites (or their content) that are not owned by the publisher.

Workman books may be purchased in bulk for business, educational, or promotional use. For information, please contact your local bookseller or the Hachette Book Group Special Markets Department at special.markets@hbgusa.com.

Library of Congress Cataloging-in-Publication Data is available.

ISBN 978-1-5235-2566-9

First Edition May 2025

Printed in China on responsibly sourced paper.

10 9 8 7 6 5 4 3 2 1

To Rais,

who now loves eating plants.

Contents

Preface

I am not a strictly vegan cook or plant-based eater, but that doesn't stop me from folding centuries' worth of plant-based culinary traditions and techniques into my own home cooking. Southern plant-based cooking is no longer a contradictory concept. Satisfying bowls of mac and cheese can be just as creamy and decadent when made plant based. Flaky biscuits can keep their distinct layers from masterful technique alone, irrespective of their source of fat.

Growing up in and eating my way through the South taught me to pay close attention to silky textures and delicately layered flavors. Learning to cook with more plants has strengthened my ability to re-create Southern food memories with just as much comfort in every bite.

Nomadically raised in the southeastern United States, I collected homes in Southern states like notches on a belt: I was born in Alabama and trailed through Texas, Kentucky, and Tennessee until my family eventually settled, and I started my life of food memories in Marietta, Georgia. Like most people who have never lived in the South, I only understood the rich culinary history through a cloudy lens that zoomed in on indulgent plates of fried fish or second helpings of beefy shepherd's pie—perhaps because Southern recipes were my family's way of experiencing indulgence outside of the plant-loving South Asian dishes we routinely ate in our Bangladeshi household. We'd celebrate good grades with all-you-can-eat fried chicken at Golden Corral or early morning fried chicken biscuits from Chick-fil-A.

It wasn't until I left the South as an adult that I began to explore the diverse decadence my Southern roots had to offer.

When I was young and ungrateful, fresh sweet corn on the cob was just corn in my eyes—the ubiquitous side dish. It never occurred to me that one day I would seek out this humble crop and cherish each kernel on a summer-ripened ear like jewels on a crown. My appreciation for the South's vibrant and readily available selection of produce didn't peak until my naïveté ran up against the cutthroat timeline that is "tomato season" in New York City—where finding a tomato that has more flavor than water is simply not guaranteed. Every time I begrudgingly pay $5 a pop for a candy-colored farmers market tomato, I can't help but dwell on memories of my mom's garden-grown beefsteaks, with which I'd make a ruby-red tomato sandwiches nearly six months out of the year.

Writing this book is the closest I can get to time-traveling back to the memories that first inspired my taste buds. Each recipe is designed to make plant-based methods feel as beginner friendly as possible, whether you live a plant-based life or not. More plant-based chefs and recipe developers than ever spend their time testing new techniques and evolving the old ones. The result? Re-creating the foods that you love with more plants. It's easy to read a cookbook as a collection of successful recipes, but I hope you realize that this book, more than anything, is an amalgamation of the trial and error process that is cooking, and that I've perfected the recipes here for you. The recipes should teach you how to not only cook Southern dishes but also calibrate your intuitive cooking habits to harness plants for their inherently impressive flavors and textures in comfort cooking. Learning to cook Southern food with more plants isn't a limitation, but rather an opportunity to open the floodgates of smarter skills and techniques in everyday home cooking.

Mebreen Karim

Introduction

Southern cooking is a rich tapestry of flavors and textures that evolved over centuries, influenced by threads of Native American, European, African, and Caribbean culinary traditions, overlaid with the influences of regional ingredients and historical events. Native Americans introduced European settlers to crops like corn, squash, and beans, which became staples in Southern cuisine. The recipes in this book celebrate these very crops and their sustainable origins while simultaneously honoring historical cooking techniques, spices, and ingredients that millions of enslaved Africans laid as the bedrock of Southern cooking. Over time, these cultural influences from African Americans and European colonial powers adapted to the local climate and resources, leading to the creation of the distinctive Southern home-cooked flair we know and crave today.

Traditionally, the use of dairy, poultry, and pork products has defined many Southern dishes. From the earliest days of colonization, Southern food traditions were influenced by European settlers who brought their animal-centric culinary practices to the region. The abundance of fertile land made it conducive to livestock farming, and Southern farmers raised cattle, hogs, and poultry in large numbers. This accessibility of meat sources led to the development of a cuisine where meat became a cornerstone ingredient.

Among the most iconic Southern dishes is fried chicken, a favorite example of a satisfying crispy, golden-brown treat. And a fried chicken meal wouldn't be complete without a sweet slab of buttery cornbread. Every bite satiates a textural craving and leaves you waiting eagerly for the next. However, characterizing Southern cuisine as only fried chicken, glazed ribs, and cornbread does a severe disservice to the infinite possibilities of its range. Not only can these flavors and textures be re-created with plants, but the core of Southern food and cooking can easily be adapted with plant-based techniques.

Learning to cook plant-powered Southern food is no more difficult than simply adopting some basic ingredients into your pantry and fridge and learning how to utilize their unique properties. Luscious creamed greens (page 44) don't sacrifice any flavor or richness when you lean into using coconut milk and top the cooked greens with crispy garlic chips. Fried green tomatoes (page 47) require no egg for binding but instead can be made with a cheap and easy-to-find alternative—chickpea flour. Instead of attempting to re-create a typical slice of cornbread, a simple plant-based twist enlists frozen corn, canned creamed corn (which, shockingly, is vegan!), and a homemade vegetarian cornbread mix. The result is a moist-on-the-inside, crispy-on-the-outside cornbread casserole that doesn't pretend to be what it's not. Like many of the recipes in this book, Cornbread Casserole (page 37) harnesses the power of plant-based products and uses them to make an evolved yet simple version of the original dish.

Equip yourself with some simple tricks to achieve ultimate creaminess in classic Southern plant-based comfort dishes. Boil and blend cashews to make a creamy base for a quick Mushroom and Potato Pot Pie Casserole (page 65) or Summer Squash Casserole (page 80). Add chickpea flour to thicken Creamy Chickpea Noodle Soup (page 93). Soft silken tofu, in its innate, creamy form, can transform into a creamy spinach hand pie filling (page 60), a mayonnaise substitute (page 151) you'll keep slathering on all your tomato toasts, or even the base of a chocolate cream pie (page 126).

Plant-based Southern food doesn't automatically entail direct copycats of traditional Southern recipes, either. Indulge in some unconventional, Southern-inspired recipes such as Creamy Labneh and Spiced Peach Dip (page 49) or Pimento Cheese Pasta (page 73). By harnessing the South's native produce in creative ways, these plant-based recipes celebrate readily available veggies and ingredients while teaching you how to transform them into easy and comforting dishes.

The world of meat alternatives is as expansive as ever, and some prove to mimic meaty textures surprisingly well. However, you don't need to buy a ground meat substitute to cook plant based. Instead, swap in produce like eggplant and marvel at its delightfully meaty bite in the BBQ Eggplant and Slaw Sandwich (page 87). Embrace mushrooms' natural umami and tender flesh to make a vegan fried "chicken" sandwich (page 77). The textures and inherent flavors of everyday ingredients will not only improve your ability to cook plant-based dishes but also elevate your understanding of humble ingredients and their application across any cuisine.

Whether you practice plant-based eating or not, there's no doubt that the arc of the world's eating habits is bending toward plants. According to a report by GlobalData, the number of self-identified vegans around the world increased by over 600 percent from 2014 to 2017. This book is perfect for anyone who wants to learn how to re-create nostalgic, Southern-inspired foods well, with love and without animal products. Each recipe is a lesson in strategizing with your ingredients before you even begin cooking, with tips like making garlic paste in bulk or turning store-bought jam into a spicy chutney. Instead of asking you to stock up on all fresh or raw ingredients, I show you how to make delicious Southern dishes using canned goods or frozen ingredients wherever possible. You will learn to cook stunning dishes with ingredients that you can buy ahead of time and experiment with whenever your heart desires.

In order to get the most out of cooking this book, don't be afraid to taste and adjust flavors as you go. The recipes as they are will guarantee a flavorful outcome, but you can also customize the recipes based on your favorite flavors and whoever you're cooking for. Many recipes come with a "Freestyle It" section dedicated to teaching you how to choose your own adventure depending on the ingredients you have on hand, or a "Meal-ify It" option for when you want to turn a recipe into complete lunch or dinner, either by adding simple ingredients or pairing it with other dishes in this book. These recipes aren't just for enjoying in the peace of your own solitude, either—they are intended for you to indulge in and cherish with your loved ones across a dinner table or over the kitchen counter. You and your guests will marvel at how easy it is to cook impressive, yet good ole comfort food that just happens to be plant powered.

Keep Your Kitchen Stocked

Stock your kitchen with essential ingredients the same way an artist equips themself with fundamental paint colors. Keep in mind, though: Painters don't keep every paint in every shade of the rainbow with them at all times; they learn to mix and create the shades they need out of a few base colors. So consider this a list of staple ingredients to help you cook and blend the vivid colors found in a Southern palette. Understanding the versatility of your pantry ingredients will allow you to cook and customize these plant-based recipes with ease and intuition. Not every ingredient is traditionally Southern, but they are effective shortcuts and building blocks for classic Southern flavors and textures, indeed.

PANTRY

CANNED AND DRIED BEANS

Never take beans, in all their cheap, nutritious, shelf-stable glory, for granted. Keep your pantry stocked with a variety of canned chickpeas, butter beans, and black beans so you can be flexible when deciding which you want to simmer in your pasta sauce or slow-cook into a hearty stew. Some beans I prefer to keep dried, like black-eyed peas, a nutritious and historically Southern staple. They don't need to be soaked before you cook them into a simple stew. Keeping a variety of beans on hand won't break the bank but will equip you with a range of options when figuring out dinner.

CHICKPEA FLOUR (BESAN)

It's nearly impossible to think about plant-based dishes without referring to chickpea flour. Chickpea flour, also known as gram flour or besan, is derived from ground chickpeas and is a textural powerhouse when cooking any type of plant-based meal. Its unique binding properties make it a great addition to soups, savory bakes, and fritters, doing the work an egg otherwise would. Plus it's a fantastic yet background source of protein. While brands like Bob's Red Mill offer chickpea flour, nothing beats the value—or flavor—of a bag of gram flour or besan from your local South Asian grocery store.

GROUND FLAXSEED

Ground flaxseed, often hailed as a superfood, plays a vital role in vegan baking, offering myriad benefits that contribute to the success of plant-based recipes. When mixed with water, it forms a gel-like consistency, akin to the binding properties of eggs. This gel not only binds ingredients but also provides moisture, helping achieve that desirable texture in baked goods. This egg replacement is crucial for creating structure and stability in vegan recipes, from cakes and cookies to muffins and pancakes.

MAPLE SYRUP

Cooking and baking recipes can be adjusted and centered on maple syrup's delicious, nutty flavor. It's important to balance savory dishes with a touch of sweetness, but sugar injects one-dimensional sweetness into dishes and also requires heat and time to dissolve into foods. Reach for maple syrup the next time you make barbecue sauce or banana bread.

NUTRITIONAL YEAST

Vegan home cooks have been on the "nooch" train since the 1970s, dousing roast veggies and dairy-free pizzas with this convenient cheese-flavored seasoning. Nutritional yeast is not only a flavor enhancer but also a valuable source of essential nutrients including B vitamins, protein, and minerals like zinc and magnesium. Its rich, cheesy flavor and nutritional value makes it particularly appealing to those following a plant-based diet. Keep a jar in your cupboard to sprinkle on crispy tofu, or blend a handful into mac and cheese sauce.

NEUTRAL OIL

Recipes that call for "neutral oil" give you the liberty to choose whichever oil works best for you. Oils like vegetable, canola, and avocado are neutral in flavor. Which one you choose may come down to price and smoke point. For everyday cooking, invest in avocado oil. Its high smoke point is great for searing veggies, and its neutral flavor works great in sauces and dressings. For baking, you can lean on cheaper varieties like vegetable or canola oil. They add no flavor to cakes but will help keep them moist for days.

TOMATO PASTE

You can never have too much tomato paste on hand. In its deep, reduced, undiluted state, tomato paste is a natural source of umami due to its concentration of glutamate, an amino acid responsible for that savory sensation. As the base of sauces and stews, frying down tomato paste will leave dishes tasting robust and full bodied. You'll typically find it in a can, but seek out a tube so that you can reseal it and not have to worry about storing an open metal can. A small amount goes a long way, allowing you to achieve that deep umami flavor without needing to use excessive quantities. Instead of spending hours simmering tomatoes to achieve a rich flavor base, you can simply reach for tomato paste, and reduce cooking time significantly.

FREEZER

CASHEWS
Cashews' soft texture and high fat content (shout out to monounsaturated fats!) make them the key to the creamy mouthfeel you want in plant-based sauces and gravies. When boiled and blended, cashews emulsify to a consistency that mimics traditional dairy-based products. Unlike other nuts, raw cashews are nearly flavorless, making them an ideal blank canvas for any flavors you wish to impart to cashew cream. Cashews' creamy and mild nature makes them a reliable base for other ingredients to take center stage. Buying cashews in bulk? Freeze them in an airtight bag to retain their freshness.

MEDIUM-FIRM, FIRM, AND EXTRA FIRM TOFU
Tofu is an extraordinarily popular ingredient in sides and main dishes across the globe for good reason—it's porous and nearly flavorless, making it a versatile vehicle for any flavors or textures you crave. As soon as you bring extra firm tofu home from the store, throw the package into the freezer until you're ready to use it. As the water within the tofu crystallizes and expands upon freezing, it creates pockets that give the tofu a more chewy, spongy texture when thawed. Added bonus:

Thawed frozen tofu requires much less time to press the water out. Expanding the gaps of air inside the tofu makes for a lighter piece of tofu that effortlessly surrenders its excess water with a few gentle pats with a towel.

PUFF PASTRY
The classic Pepperidge Farm brand of frozen puff pastry contains no animal products, making it completely plant based. There are vegan-branded puff pastry products out there as well, so the options for getting a flaky crust on pot pies are varied. Keeping a box of puff pastry sheets in your freezer will save you time and effort for your next dinner party. Package any savory or sweet filling in different shapes of pastry and end up with unique sides and desserts even when you're in a rush.

FRIDGE

PLANT-BASED BUTTER
Technology and innovation pushed the needle on plant-based dairy products when plant-based (vegan) butters entered the market. Plant-based butters are an emulsified blend of oils and stabilizers that replicates dairy butter's function in cooking and baking. Now you can choose from a selection of butters designed to be spread straight onto bread or baked into a pie crust. EarthBalance provides a variety of plant-based butters, all varying in their uses

and allergen content. It will work in any application at a much lower price than other plant-based butters. Feel free to choose whichever works best for your lifestyle and use it as you would regular dairy butter.

MISO

Whether you cook entirely plant based or not, every home cook needs a tub of white miso sitting in their fridge. Packed with concentrated notes of umami and saltiness, this fermented soybean paste lends a depth of flavor to whatever you use it in. Blend miso into a handful of ingredients to create a surprisingly simple Magic Mayo (page 151) that mimics the umami you'd normally taste in egg-based mayo. When you keep this flavor bomb handy, you'll get added complexity in all dishes, both savory and sweet. Throw it into dressings and glazes, or use as the base of soups and stews. Find miso in the refrigerated section of your local grocery store or Asian market.

OAT MILK

Oat milk boasts a subtle and neutral flavor profile. Unlike soy and almond milk, it doesn't overpower the other flavors in recipes. This neutrality allows the primary flavors of dishes to shine, making it an excellent base for a wide range of recipes. Oat milk's natural creaminess is a significant advantage in plant-based cooking and baking. You can use it to

create a makeshift vegan buttermilk that will successfully add tang and rise to pancakes. Cook it into sauces to give them a luscious texture without the need for added thickeners or stabilizers.

SOFT SILKEN TOFU

Silken tofu—the shapeshifting star of all the pantry items—is a delicate and soft tofu created by curdling soy milk without much agitation, resulting in a high moisture content and a smooth, custard-like texture. For plant-based cooking, it's a creamy cheat code you can use in shakes, pasta sauces, puddings, and dressings.

PLANT-BASED CHORIZO

Plant-based chorizo, made with soy, can be used for so much more than Spanish- and Mexican-inspired dishes that traditionally employ chorizo. Plant-based chorizo masterfully captures the complex taste of its meat-based counterpart, serving as a one-stop shop for flavor thanks to its blend of spices including paprika, cumin, and chile, and its characteristic smokiness. That means less work for you and guaranteed flavor for anything you throw it into. Keep a few packages in your fridge for last-minute gravies, tacos, or stews. There are plenty of plant-based chorizo brands and types to choose from at your local grocery store.

Breakfast & Brunch

Start your day with playful twists on hearty breakfast classics. Southern brunch dishes balance both savory and sweet flavors as an art form, so there's something in this batch for everyone to satisfy their morning or all-day cravings. From fluffy pancakes to—of course—a flaky biscuit, these simple techniques and common ingredients will help build your plant-based cooking confidence.

Crispy Lemony Breakfast Potatoes

Mastering the crispy-outside/fluffy-inside breakfast potato will change mornings as you know them. While you might be tempted to skip the parboil, it's nonnegotiable in this recipe. Baking raw potato cubes will give them a denser interior and a papery outer layer of "crispiness" that will grow soggy in minutes. But parboiling the spuds first will temper the potato's starchiness and allow the potatoes to form a crust that crisps up in the oven—and stays crisp. The lemon-basil dressing introduces a much-welcome pop of bright Mediterranean flavors that pair beautifully with any morning savories.

SERVES 4

¼ cup (60 ml) olive oil

1½ pounds (675 g) all-purpose potatoes (preferably Yukon Gold or new), scrubbed

2 tablespoons kosher salt

½ teaspoon baking soda

1½ teaspoons black pepper

2 tablespoons freshly squeezed lemon juice

½ packed cup (30 g) fresh basil leaves (see Freestyle It)

2 garlic cloves, peeled, or 1 teaspoon Garlic Paste (page 163)

Grated zest of 1 lemon

Preheat the oven to 450°F (230°C). Line a large baking sheet with aluminum foil and drizzle with 1 tablespoon of the olive oil.

Cut the potatoes into 1- to 2-inch (2 to 5 cm) pieces. Fill a large pot with water and add the potatoes, salt, and baking soda. Set the pot over medium-high heat and bring to a rolling boil. Once the water is vigorously bubbling, reduce the heat to low and cover the pot, leaving the lid slightly ajar for steam to escape. Simmer the potatoes for another 7 to 8 minutes, until a fork can pierce a potato with little resistance.

Drain the potatoes and place them in a large mixing bowl. Add 2 tablespoons of the remaining olive oil, pepper, and 1 tablespoon of the lemon juice.

(continued)

Use a large spoon or shake the bowl to toss the potatoes around with the seasonings. Discard any potato peels that naturally fall off.

Spread out the potatoes on the prepared baking sheet and place in the oven. After 25 minutes, remove the potatoes from the oven and shake the pan or flip the potatoes with a spatula. (This will ensure that all sides of the potatoes crisp up.) Return the potatoes to the oven and roast for another 30 minutes, or until the potatoes are golden brown on all sides.

While the potatoes are roasting, finely chop the basil and add it to a small glass jar or bowl. Use a Microplane to grate the garlic cloves directly into the jar, or add the garlic paste. Add a pinch of salt, the remaining tablespoon olive oil, the remaining tablespoon lemon juice, and the lemon zest. If using a jar, cover it tightly with its lid and shake. If using a bowl, stir vigorously with a small whisk or fork until the dressing is completely emulsified. Drizzle the lemon-basil dressing over the roasted potatoes and shake to distribute. Finish the potatoes with another pinch of salt and serve while warm.

Freestyle It

> Any fresh herb, such as cilantro, parsley, or dill, is welcome in this recipe so long as you like how it tastes with lemon!

Saucy Tomato Tofu and Grits

This pared-down, but no less flavorful, take on shrimp and grits makes for a low-stress, high-reward bowl of breakfast. The best part? Both components of this dish are easy to store for a future dinner.

SERVES 4 TO 6

1 package (14 ounces/397 g) extra firm or firm tofu

2 tablespoons olive oil

1 large red onion, peeled

4 garlic cloves, peeled, or 2 teaspoons Garlic Paste (page 163)

4 teaspoons kosher salt

½ teaspoon smoked sweet paprika

½ teaspoon ground turmeric

½ teaspoon red pepper flakes

1 can (28 ounces/794 g) whole peeled San Marzano tomatoes

1 tablespoon soy sauce

1 teaspoon brown sugar

1 carton (32 ounces/907 g) low-sodium vegetable broth

1 cup (150 g) quick-cooking grits

1 tablespoon nutritional yeast

Unsweetened plant-based milk (optional)

½ packed cup (30 g) chopped fresh parsley, basil, or cilantro

Pat the tofu dry with a paper towel and break it into ½- to 1-inch (1 to 2 cm) pieces by hand. Add the olive oil to a large nonstick skillet over medium heat. Once the oil is hot and shimmering, add the tofu and fry for 10 to 12 minutes, stirring and flipping the pieces about every 3 minutes, until golden brown and crisp. Transfer the tofu to a paper towel–lined plate.

Thinly slice the onion and the garlic cloves, if using. Add the onions to the skillet, along with more olive oil if it's dry. Use a wooden spoon or silicone spatula to stir the onions for 2 to 3 minutes, until just softened. Add the garlic, 1 teaspoon of the salt, the paprika, turmeric, and red pepper flakes and stir until the garlic slices are soft and the spices have begun to brown, about 2 minutes. Stir in the tomatoes and their juice along with the soy sauce and brown sugar. Simmer over medium-low heat for at least 10 minutes, stirring occasionally to break up the tomatoes.

(continued)

While the sauce is simmering, bring 3 cups (720 ml) of the vegetable broth, 2½ cups (590 ml) water, and the remaining 3 teaspoons salt to a boil in a large saucepan over medium heat. Pour in the grits and whisk to combine while everything comes back to a boil. Once the water is vigorously bubbling, reduce the heat to low. Stir the grits every few minutes, making sure to scrape the bottom of the pan. After about 5 minutes, the grits will thicken to a loose, pudding-like consistency. Dip a clean spatula or wooden spoon into the grits and check if they cling to the spatula without running. If they immediately run off, continue cooking for another minute, then check again. Take the grits off the heat and stir in the nutritional yeast. Cover and set aside to keep warm.

Taste the sauce and add more salt or other seasoning to your preference. Add the crispy tofu to the sauce and let the tofu soak up the sauce over low heat for at least 5 minutes.

Check the consistency of the grits again before serving. Stir in a few tablespoons milk if the grits are thicker than a wet cake batter. Divide the grits into deep bowls, spoon over the saucy tofu, and garnish with the herb or herbs of your choice.

Freestyle It

› For extra heft, add a can of chickpeas or handful of greens to the sauce along with the tofu—this recipe is made for personalizing.

Grits Take Us Back to the Future

Grits, a culinary mascot of the American South, hold a lineage far older than America itself. As early as 7,000 years ago, Mayans, Aztecs, and Incas utilized advanced agricultural techniques to grow and process corn to make the nutrients more accessible. This process, which is known as nixtamalization, involves soaking the corn kernels in an alkaline solution to soften the hull. This ancient technique not only improves the digestibility and nutritional value of corn but also led to the creation of grits, which are a sustainable staple in Indigenous, African American, and American Southern diets.

European settlers quickly adopted Native American culinary sustenance such as grits and began incorporating it into their diets—they were not only a reliable food source but also a versatile ingredient that could be prepared in various ways. During the South's antebellum era, grits were commonly cooked by enslaved Africans who were brought to the Southern states. The cultural exchange between African and European culinary traditions contributed to the evolution of Southern cuisine, with grits becoming a symbol of comfort, community, and flavor.

Today, grits remain an enduring Southern icon, adopted by all Southerners as a favorite. Grits have evolved from a simple sustenance food to a versatile canvas for culinary creativity. Chefs and home cooks alike experiment with flavors and toppings, adding their own twists to classic recipes. Grits are a cherished part of the Southern culinary tapestry, embodying the warmth and hospitality native to the Southern spirit. In their humble glory, grits take center stage in innovative dishes such as cheesy grits soufflés, crispy grits cakes, and even grits-based desserts. This evolution speaks to the resilience and adaptability of native foods, showcasing their ability to remain relevant in a rapidly changing culinary landscape.

Broiled Peach and Oatmeal Bake

There's no shame in wanting to eat dessert for breakfast, especially when it's filled with hearty, good-for-you ingredients and topped with caramelized fruit. Make this recipe ahead of a busy week so you can wake up to a convenient slice of oatmeal that tastes like a peach crumble.

SERVES 4 TO 6

4 large peaches

3 tablespoons coconut oil, melted

¾ cup (about 90 g) toasted pistachios, walnuts, or pecans

1½ cups (360 ml) unsweetened plant-based milk, plus more if needed

2 tablespoons maple syrup

1 tablespoon ground flaxseed

1 teaspoon baking powder

1 teaspoon ground cinnamon

1 teaspoon pure vanilla extract

½ teaspoon kosher salt

½ teaspoon ground ginger

¼ teaspoon ground nutmeg

2 cups (200 g) old-fashioned oats

1 tablespoon brown sugar

Plant-based yogurt, for serving

Place a rack close to the broiler heating element. Set the broiler to high.

Pit and dice 2 of the peaches and set aside in a large mixing bowl. Pit and slice the remaining 2 peaches into 6 to 8 slices per peach. Toss the peach slices with 1 tablespoon of the coconut oil in a metal 9 × 9-inch (23 × 23 cm) baking pan. Place the pan on the rack under the broiler and broil for 5 to 7 minutes, until the edges of the peaches are deeply browned, almost charred.

While the peaches broil, chop the pistachios.

Transfer the broiled peaches to a plate. Keep the baking pan out; you're going to use it again.

Preheat the oven to 350°F (175°C) and move an oven rack to the middle of the oven.

(continued)

Add the remaining 2 tablespoons coconut oil, the milk, maple syrup, flaxseed, baking powder, cinnamon, vanilla, salt, ginger, and nutmeg to the diced peaches. Stir until everything is evenly combined. Add the oats and ½ cup (40 g) of the chopped pistachios. If the mixture seems too thick, add more milk 1 tablespoon at a time until it reaches a thick, cake batter–like consistency.

Transfer the peach-oat mixture to the baking pan. Arrange the reserved peach slices on top. Sprinkle the rest of the pistachios around the peaches then sprinkle the brown sugar over everything.

Place the baking pan on the middle rack of the oven. Bake for 40 to 45 minutes, until the top is deep golden brown and feels set to the touch. If the top begins to brown before it feels set, gently place a large sheet of aluminum foil over the baking pan, creating a loose tent with large vents for the air to get through. The goal is to protect the surface from the oven's direct heat.

Let the oatmeal cool for 15 minutes before slicing and serving while still warm, with a spoonful of cold yogurt. Store leftovers in an airtight container in the refrigerator for up to 1 week, or in the freezer for up to month.

Flaky Biscuits and Quick Strawberry-Pepper Jam

This is the only plant-based biscuit you'll ever need. It can be dressed up with herbs, spices, and more, but I prefer its tender, savory bite with a sweet-and-spicy jam. Don't worry—making a quick jam won't take up more bandwidth than simply simmering some fruit and sugar together; it will be done by the time the biscuits are ready to serve.

MAKES 9 BISCUITS AND 1½ CUPS (475 G) JAM

STRAWBERRY-PEPPER JAM

1 pound (450 g) fresh or frozen strawberries, sliced

1 packed cup (220 g) brown sugar

½ cup (100 g) granulated sugar

2 tablespoons freshly squeezed lemon juice

½ teaspoon kosher salt

1 habanero chile

BISCUITS

4 cups (500 g) all-purpose flour, plus more for dusting

1 tablespoon baking powder

2 teaspoon baking soda

1 teaspoon kosher salt

1 cup (2 sticks/230 to 250 g) plant-based butter, frozen

4 tablespoons freshly squeezed lemon juice

1½ cup (355 ml) unsweetened oat milk, plus more for brushing

Add the strawberries, brown sugar, granulated sugar, lemon juice, and salt to a large saucepan. Slice the habanero chile in half and drop it into the saucepan. (The habanero will infuse a deep, fruity spice into the jam without overpowering the sweetness with heat.) Bring to a simmer over medium-high heat and cook for 15 to 20 minutes, stirring occasionally, until the jam has thickened and cooked down to about 1½ cups (475 g). (You can start preparing the biscuits while the jam is cooking, if you like.)

After the jam has cooked down, taste it and decide whether it is spicy enough for you. If yes, remove the habanero and use a wooden spoon

(continued)

to mash some of the strawberries down. (I prefer my jam to have some pieces of fruit remaining visible, but mash as much as you like.) If you prefer a spicier jam, use the spoon to mash the habanero into the jam, releasing its seeds. Then remove the remaining flesh of the habanero.

Lower the heat to medium and cook for another 5 minutes. If the jam coats the back of a wooden spoon, it is done. If the jam is still too runny, continue cooking for another 3 to 5 minutes, until the jam coats the back of your spoon. Transfer the jam to a jar or lidded container. Let it cool before serving or storing in the refrigerator. The jam will keep for up to 4 weeks.

For the biscuits, preheat the oven to 425°F (220°C). Line a baking sheet with parchment paper and set aside.

Add the flour, baking powder, baking soda, and salt to a large mixing bowl and whisk until fully mixed. Set aside.

Divide the butter into two equal portions. Dice half of the butter into ½-inch (1 cm) cubes. Use the largest holes on a box grater to grate the remaining butter into flaky shards. Add all the butter to the dry ingredients. Gently toss the butter pieces in the flour until they're totally covered and separate from one another. Place in the fridge to keep cold.

Add the lemon juice to the oat milk and stir until combined. Place in the fridge to chill and curdle into buttermilk.

Remove the butter-flour mixture from the fridge. Use your fingers to press and pinch the cubes of butter into flakes and eventually smaller, rolled oat–size pieces. The mixture should resemble pebbly sand.

Spread a 24 × 12-inch (60 × 30 cm) sheet of parchment paper on your work surface.

Make a well in the center of the flour-butter mixture, with some still coating the bottom of the bowl. Slowly pour half of the buttermilk into the well. Use a fork to fold in about half of the flour-butter mixture. Pour in the rest of the buttermilk and fold in the second half of the flour-butter mixture. Once mostly combined, use your hands to transfer the dough onto the parchment paper.

Press the clumps of dough together into a mountain. (Keep extra flour handy in case the dough is too sticky to handle.) Try not to knead the dough, just pat it into a 9 × 9-inch (23 × 23 cm) square. Cut the square into quarters and stack them on top of each other. Use your hands and a floured rolling pin to pat the stacked squares back into a 9 × 9-inch (23 × 23 cm) square. (This lamination process will ensure flaky layers; just don't overwork the dough or it will become tough.) If at any point you notice that the butter is melting or the dough is tough, cover the dough with a clean kitchen towel or plastic wrap and transfer it, still on the parchment paper, to the refrigerator to rest for 10 minutes. Once the dough has been reshaped into the large square, cover it and transfer to rest in the refrigerator for 10 minutes before slicing and baking.

Place the dough on a cutting board and slice it into 9 equal squares. Arrange the biscuits on the lined baking sheet and brush the tops with oat milk. Bake for 15 to 20 minutes, until the tops are light golden brown. Serve warm with the jam.

To store any leftover biscuits, place them in a resealable bag or airtight container and refrigerate for up to 4 days, or freeze for up to 1 month. To reheat frozen biscuits, sprinkle them with a few drops of water and wrap them in aluminum foil before warming them in the oven at 350°F (175°C) for 6 to 8 minutes, or until they are warm to the touch.

Freestyle It

> Pair these biscuits with a mushroom-studded gravy like the one on page 155 for a proper Southern-style breakfast, or make some chicken-fried mushroom patties (page 77) for some plant-based chicken biscuits.

Building a Better Biscuit

It's difficult to make a truly *bad* biscuit. Flour, salt, and loads of fat rarely result in a totally undesirable product. But making a good, no, *better* biscuit than you get at a bakery, restaurant, or your grandma's house is indeed tricky. All ovens, flours, and butters are different, so no one recipe will work the same for all bakers. Here are some keys to pay attention to in order to truly make your biscuits better—if not the best you've ever had.

GRATE AND CUBE THE BUTTER

This biscuit recipe calls for dicing half of the butter and grating the remaining half on the large holes of a box grater. And the butter is frozen beforehand. Grating frozen butter creates long, flat shards that will guarantee distribution throughout the dough. When the biscuits bake, these shards melt and immediately release steam, causing the biscuit dough to rise, creating a flaky biscuit. Cubing the butter, then pressing it with your fingers, yields larger and varied sizes of shards that accomplish the same goal but contribute even larger pockets of steam. Together, both the grated and cubed pieces of butter form a fluffy biscuit with a variety of aerated moments within.

KEEP IT CHILL

All biscuit recipes will remind you to chill the butter beforehand, but there's no harm in repeating how important this is. Freeze the butter ahead of time, and keep the mixed butter and flour in the fridge too, especially if the environment is on the warmer side (anywhere above 68°F/20°C). Feel free to throw the biscuit mix into the fridge after each step to ensure the butter doesn't melt along the way: after mixing the butter into the flour, after mixing the buttermilk into the dough, and after shaping the dough into a square.

FLAVOR THE FLOUR

Baking is a great way to experiment with ingredients and flavors, especially if you keep your eye on proportions. So long as you don't add a huge extra volume of dry ingredients to these biscuits, you can infuse them with infinite flavor combinations. Try a combination of warm spices in the flour mix, like smoked sweet paprika, cumin, ginger, or turmeric. Adding dried herbs is another creative way to add texture and flavor to biscuits.

Fluffy Cardamom-Blueberry Pancakes

Pancakes don't need eggs to be fluffy and aerated. Before you start on the pancake batter, make a simple cardamom-infused coconut oil that you'll fry the pancakes in. Infusing the coconut oil will delicately incorporate cardamom flavor into the pancakes but not overpower the dish.

SERVES 3 OR 4

½ cup (120 g) refined coconut oil

6 green or white cardamom pods

1¾ cups (415 ml) unsweetened oat milk

2 tablespoons freshly squeezed lemon juice or apple cider vinegar

½ cup (120 ml) full-fat coconut milk, at room temperature

2 cups (250 g) all-purpose flour

2 tablespoons granulated sugar

1½ tablespoons baking powder

½ teaspoon kosher salt

1 pint (275 g) fresh blueberries

Maple syrup, for serving

Set a small saucepan over medium heat and add the coconut oil. Break open the cardamom pods and add the seeds to the oil; discard the outer pods. Swirl the pan as the oil comes to a simmer and the seeds start to release bubbles, about 3 minutes. Let simmer over low heat for another 5 minutes, or until the oil smells deeply of cardamom. Remove the pan from the heat and pour the infused oil through a fine-mesh sieve into a small heatproof jar or container. Discard the cardamom pods and seeds.

Stir together the oat milk and lemon juice in a medium bowl. Let the milk curdle for about 5 minutes to become buttermilk. Add the coconut milk and stir again. Pour in 2 tablespoons of the infused oil and stir to combine. (The rest of the infused oil will be used for frying the pancakes.)

Combine the flour, sugar, baking powder, and salt in a large mixing bowl. Pour the liquid ingredients into the dry ingredients and gently stir with a silicone spatula or wooden spoon. The batter should be clumpy, but with

(continued)

no large clods of dry flour; it is better to undermix than overmix the batter in this case. Set the batter aside to rest for 5 to 10 minutes, to relax any gluten that has formed. If you notice clumps of dry flour after resting, use a small spoon to break up just the clumps, rather than mixing everything together.

Pour 1 tablespoon of the infused oil into a large nonstick skillet and set it over medium heat. Once you can smell the oil's aroma, use a ladle to scoop ¼ to ⅓ cup (about 40 g) of the batter into the skillet for as many pancakes as will fit. Use a silicone spatula to push the oil around the edges of the pancakes. Scatter a handful of blueberries on top of each. Cook for 2 to 3 minutes, until the edges and underside are deep golden brown. Flip and cook the second side for another 2 to 3 minutes, until the edges appear set. To preserve the fluffiness, don't flip the pancakes more than once! Either serve each pancake fresh or set them aside on a baking sheet to serve all at once.

Cook the remaining pancakes, adding another tablespoon of the infused oil to the pan if it looks dry. Serve with maple syrup, a drizzle of the infused oil, and the remainder of the blueberries.

Mushroom and Soy Chorizo Hash

Plant-based chorizo is filled with seemingly endless flavor, making it the perfect key to a robustly spiced and seasoned breakfast hash with minimal ingredients. Don't wince at the use of ketchup here—it's a simple way of injecting the hash with both more umami and a touch of sugar to balance out the warmth of the plant-based chorizo.

SERVES 4

1 large yellow or white onion, peeled

1 pound (450 g) portobello or white mushrooms

2 cups (140 g) chopped kale leaves

12 ounces (340 g) plant-based chorizo (any brand), crumbled

2 scallions, trimmed

¼ cup (60 ml) olive oil

3½ cups (450 g) frozen shredded hash brown potatoes, thawed

1 teaspoon kosher salt

½ teaspoon black pepper

3 garlic cloves, peeled, or 1½ teaspoons Garlic Paste (page 163)

2 tablespoons ketchup

1 teaspoon soy sauce

Chop the onion into ½- to 1-inch (1 to 2 cm) pieces and set aside. Wipe the mushrooms clean with a paper towel and cut them into ¼-inch-thick (6 mm) slices. Add the mushrooms, kale, and plant-based chorizo to a medium bowl and set aside. Thinly slice the scallions into rings and set aside separately.

Set a large stainless-steel or cast-iron skillet over medium heat and add 2 tablespoons of the olive oil. Once the oil is shimmering and hot, add the potatoes. Use a wooden spoon or silicone spatula to distribute the potatoes across the skillet, making sure they completely cover the base of the skillet. Let the potatoes fry undisturbed for 8 to 10 minutes, until they are golden brown on the underside.

Stir the potatoes and then spread them out again and let them fry for another 4 to 5 minutes. Repeat stirring and spreading once more, until

(continued)

the potatoes are mostly browned all over. Season with a large pinch each of the salt and pepper and transfer the potatoes to a paper towel–lined plate.

Add the remaining 2 tablespoons olive oil to the skillet and set it over medium heat. Add the onions and stir for 2 minutes, or until the onions have softened. Use a Microplane to grate the garlic cloves directly into the skillet, or add the garlic paste. Continue to cook and stir for another 2 minutes, or until the garlic is fragrant and lightly browned. Add the ketchup, soy sauce, and the remaining salt and pepper and continue to cook, frying down the ketchup until it is a deep maroonish-brown, about 4 minutes.

Add ¼ cup (60 ml) water and the plant-based chorizo, mushrooms, and kale. Stir everything together, allowing the plant-based chorizo and mushrooms to soak up and cook in the sauce. Cook for about 5 minutes, until the mushrooms are tender and most of the water has evaporated.

Reduce the heat to low. Transfer the potatoes back into the skillet and gently toss everything together with a silicone spatula. Taste and adjust the seasoning to your preference. Sprinkle with the scallions and serve warm.

Note: To make ahead, follow the directions up until adding the potatoes to the hash mixture. Both the potatoes and hash can be made ahead and stored in the fridge, then reheated following the directions in the last step.

Carrot Cake Smoothie

Before judging this smoothie by its name, let it be known that this recipe isn't a weak attempt to trick you into making a nutritious drink by titling it after a dessert. Rather, it's a celebration of the carrot's distinct versatility in all shapes and forms—whether grated into a cake, sliced for a veggie platter, or pureed for a smoothie. Carrots' natural sweetness harmonizes with frozen banana and mango's subtly creamy texture when blended and takes on the warm aromas of cinnamon and vanilla—just like a carrot cake does.

SERVES 2

1 large carrot (about 2 ounces/55 g), scrubbed but not peeled

1 cup (140 g) frozen mango chunks

½ banana, frozen

½ cup (120 ml) full-fat coconut milk

½ cup (120 ml) ice-cold water

½ teaspoon ground cinnamon

½ teaspoon pure vanilla extract

Chop the carrot into three large chunks. Place the carrot, mango, banana, coconut milk, water, cinnamon, and vanilla in a blender and blend on high speed until smooth, about 3 minutes. Pour into two glasses and serve immediately.

Starters & Sides

Sometimes sides and appetizers are just as delicious as, if not more than, the main dish. These supporting dishes successfully balance any meal whether the menu is in need of a vibrant salad or a creamy dip. Many of these simple yet impressive small plates can even be turned into full meals.

Cornbread Casserole

The best cornbread I've ever tasted or made always included a store-bought boxed mix in some shape or form. But since most mainstream brands of cornbread mix contain lard or animal fats in their ingredients, this recipe replaces the mix with a few simple ingredients to re-create that classic cornbread taste in the form of a creamy, scoopable casserole. The secret ingredient: canned creamed corn, which surprisingly is plant based and made with starches that will stabilize the casserole and prevent it from turning into corn mush.

SERVES 4 TO 6

1 tablespoon (15 g) plant-based butter, cold

1 cup (130 g) yellow cornmeal

1 cup (125 g) all-purpose flour

1½ teaspoons kosher salt

2 teaspoons baking powder

1 teaspoon red pepper flakes

½ teaspoon baking soda

½ teaspoon smoked sweet paprika

½ teaspoon black pepper

½ cup (1 stick/115 to 125 g) plant-based butter, plus more for greasing the dish

2 cans (14.75 ounces/418 g each) cream-style corn

1 cup (170 g) fresh or frozen corn kernels

½ packed cup (110 g) brown sugar

¼ cup (60 ml) unsweetened oat milk

1 tablespoon freshly squeezed lemon juice

3 or 4 scallions, trimmed

Preheat the oven to 350°F (175°C). Grease an 8 × 8-inch (20 × 20 cm) baking dish by rubbing the cold butter around the sides and base of the dish with your fingers. Set aside.

Add the cornmeal, flour, salt, baking powder, red pepper flakes, baking soda, paprika, and black pepper to a large mixing bowl. Whisk for 1 minute, or until the baking powder and baking soda are completely distributed. Set the dry ingredients aside.

Melt the butter in a small saucepan over medium heat or in the microwave for 30 seconds. Add the butter, cream-style corn, corn kernels, brown

(continued)

sugar, oat milk, and lemon juice to a medium mixing bowl. Whisk until smooth and the sugar begins to dissolve, 1 to 2 minutes. Add to the dry ingredients and whisk for another 2 minutes, or until no streaks of flour remain.

Slice the scallions into ¼-inch (6 mm) rings. Set aside about 2 tablespoons of the scallion greens for garnish. Add the remaining scallions to the batter and gently fold them in using a silicone spatula. Once combined, pour the batter into the prepared baking dish, scraping the sides of the bowl.

Bake for 40–45 minutes, until the top forms golden-brown spots and edges.

Let the cornbread cool in the baking dish on a wire rack for at least 10 minutes. Sprinkle the cornbread with the reserved scallions and serve immediately, while still warm.

Cover and store any leftovers in the refrigerator for up to 3 days. Single servings can be reheated in the microwave for 2 to 3 minutes. If reheating a larger portion in the casserole dish, it can be wrapped in foil and baked at 350°F (175°C) for 15 minutes.

Okra Haters, Unite

A disdain for okra's mucus-like guts is common, even in the South. However, okra's gooey seeds serve as a natural binding agent in dishes like gumbos and stir-fries, making it a critical cheat code for plant-based cooking. Instead of shunning okra's mucus, utilize its ability to bind ingredients together—a power you can take advantage of when cooking without eggs.

Okra is more versatile than you think when you cut it open to expose the seeds and cook it with care. You can use it as the main ingredient in recipes like Crispy Golden Tofu (page 52) or Fried Green Tomatoes (page 47). Just slice the okra in half lengthwise and utilize it in place of the tofu or green tomatoes in their respective recipes. The coating will cling to the seeds, which will crisp up beautifully.

Taking inspiration from everyone's favorite smashed potato recipes, Smashed Okra Fries (page 40) employs a similar method and bashes okra's slippery seeds out, then coats them with a dredge. No matter how you decide to prepare them, make sure to squeeze a bit of fresh lemon juice on your final okra dish. The brightness will immediately lift the otherwise bitter flavors you might be expecting from the okra.

Smashed Okra Fries

If the texture of okra has never appealed to you, this recipe is for you. There are three steps involved: smashing, shaking, and baking. Banging on okra in a resealable bag and shaking it around with a few pantry ingredients lets those gooey seeds escape, coats the okra in a flavorful dredge, and allows each edge to crisp up while baking in the oven.

SERVES 2 TO 4

3 tablespoons olive oil

12 ounces (340 g) fresh okra pods

2 tablespoons cornstarch

2 tablespoons unsweetened plant-based milk

1½ teaspoons kosher salt

1 teaspoon garlic powder

¼ teaspoon granulated sugar

1 lemon, cut into wedges

Magic Mayo (page 151) or other dipping sauce, for serving

Preheat the oven to 400°F (205°C). Line a baking sheet with aluminum foil and grease it with 1 tablespoon of the olive oil.

Trim off any stems left on the wide ends of the okra. Transfer the okra to a gallon-size resealable bag. Place a kitchen towel on the counter to pad it and lay the bag flat on top. Using a rolling pin or the bottom of a glass bottle, gently hit the okra, smashing the pods just enough to break them open and expose their seeds. Don't oversmash the okra pods; you want to keep them in whole pieces.

Add the remaining 2 tablespoons olive oil, the cornstarch, milk, salt, garlic powder, and sugar to the bag. Vigorously shake the bag around, ensuring the batter is thoroughly mixed and evenly coats the okra.

Spread out the okra on the prepared baking sheet. Bake for 30 minutes, or until the coating on the okra is lightly browned and crisped. Remove the baking sheet from the oven and flip the okra over using a small offset spatula. Return the okra to the oven and bake for another 15 to 20 minutes, until evenly golden brown and crisp to the touch.

Sprinkle with an extra pinch of salt while the okra is still hot. Serve with fresh lemon wedges and a dipping sauce of your choice.

Freestyle It

› While purists may shudder, you can doctor up tomato toast however you please. Thinly slice some fresh basil and place it between the tomatoes and the toast. Or add any spices you please to the frying oil—smoked sweet paprika will give the toasts a hint of red and some warmth.

Southern-Style Tomato Toast

One of the greatest culinary inventions from the South is also the simplest: fresh garden tomatoes, a slice of white bread, and luscious mayo. Working with so few ingredients means getting the very best possible flavors and textures out of them. Instead of simply seasoning the finished toasts with black pepper, infuse the olive oil with it. Fry the bread in the infused oil, then later drizzle the bloomed black pepper on top of the toasts.

SERVES 4 TO 6

2 large ripe heirloom tomatoes

1 tablespoon kosher salt

2 tablespoons olive oil

1½ teaspoons black pepper

6 slices sourdough or white sandwich bread

½ cup (120 ml) Magic Mayo (page 151)

Wash the tomatoes and gently pat dry. Use a serrated knife to cut them crosswise into ½-inch-thick (1 cm) slices. Spread out the tomato slices on a large paper towel–lined plate and evenly sprinkle the salt across them to draw out excess moisture. Set aside in the refrigerator to chill.

Warm the olive oil in a large skillet over medium heat. Once the oil is hot and shimmering, add the pepper and fry for 30 seconds, or until you can smell the pepper's fragrance. Place 3 slices of the bread in the skillet and leave undisturbed for 2 minutes, or until the underside of the bread is lightly browned. Flip the bread and fry it for another 2 minutes. Transfer the toasts to serving plates. Repeat with the remaining slices of bread. Once all the bread is done frying, take the skillet off the heat and leave the pepper-infused oil in the pan.

Lightly pat excess juice and salt off the tomato slices with a paper towel. Spread the toasts with a generous amount of the mayo and stack tomato slices on each piece of toast. Spoon the pepper-infused olive oil over the tomatoes and serve immediately.

Last-Minute Coconut-Creamed Greens

With a single can of coconut milk, a few alliums, and 20 minutes or so, you can have a plate of flavorful and saucy greens topped with a garlic-shallot crisp. Sautéed greens can taste bitter and offer little or no textural excitement, just sogginess. Correct both of these outcomes by using full-fat coconut milk to mellow out the grassy bitterness and crisping up some of the alliums. You'll have a rich and flavor-packed side dish ready for dinner.

In a serious rush? Don't sweat the crispy garlic-shallot garnish—instead, add all the alliums to the coconut sauce and use store-bought fried shallots and/or panko breadcrumbs as the crunchy topping. (You can find fried shallots in Asian markets.)

SERVES 4

1 large bunch kale or Swiss chard (about 8 ounces/225 g) or 4 packed cups (12 ounces/340 g) baby spinach

4 large shallots, peeled

6 garlic cloves, peeled

2 tablespoons olive oil

1 tablespoon kosher salt

1 can (13.5 ounces/400 ml) full-fat coconut milk

2 tablespoons hot sauce (preferably sriracha)

1 tablespoon freshly squeezed lime juice

1 tablespoon brown sugar

½ teaspoon ground turmeric

Wash and dry the greens. If using kale or Swiss chard, remove and discard the ribs and tear the leaves into 2-inch (5 cm) pieces. (If using baby spinach, no tearing will be necessary.)

Using a sharp knife, slice the shallots crosswise into thin rings and slice the garlic cloves crosswise into thin chips. Add the olive oil, half of the shallots, and half of the garlic to a medium saucepan and set it over medium heat. (When crisping alliums, starting the fry with the pan cold allows them to heat up and release water gradually rather than start browning immediately upon hitting the hot oil and potentially burning.) Fry the shallots and garlic for 5 to 7 minutes, swirling the pan every minute to promote even frying, until golden brown. Transfer the garlic and shallots with a slotted spoon to a small paper towel–lined bowl. Sprinkle with a pinch of the salt while hot; set aside.

Add the remaining shallots and garlic to the oil in the saucepan and sauté over medium heat for 2 minutes, until they are fragrant and lightly browned. Add the remaining salt, coconut milk, hot sauce, lime juice, sugar, and turmeric and stir to combine. Bring to a boil over high heat and let cook for 5 minutes. Reduce the heat to medium and simmer for another 5 minutes until the sauce is slightly thicker and coats the back of a wooden spoon.

If you're using spinach, stir it into the coconut sauce and remove the pan from the heat; the spinach will immediately wilt and be ready to eat. If using Swiss chard, stir it into the sauce and cook over low heat for 2 minutes, until wilted, then remove from the heat. For kale, add it to the sauce and simmer for 5 minutes over medium heat, until the kale is visibly shrunken but not completely wilted. Let creamed greens sit in the pan off the heat for 5 minutes to release extra steam and slightly thicken. Garnish with garlic-shallot crisp and serve.

Meal-ify It

› Turn these greens into a hearty 30-minute meal. Drain and rinse a can of your favorite chickpeas or beans and throw them into the pot along with the coconut milk. Smash half of the beans by pressing them against the side of the pot with a wooden spoon; this will release their starches and thicken the coconut sauce into a gravy. Continue to cook according to the recipe. Ladle this hearty curry-like stew onto a bowl of steaming rice or any cooked grain you have on hand.

Fried Green Tomatoes and Tangy Basil Mayo

Green tomatoes are some of summer's finest produce—they're flavorful yet uniquely sturdy, making them a great contender for frying. Resourceful Southerners in the nineteenth century fried underripe green tomatoes when ripe tomatoes were inaccessible. The fried green tomatoes provided a delicious use of the crop before they ripened into red tomatoes. Making a plant-based version of the classic dish substitutes for the usual eggy coating by dipping the slices in a chickpea flour batter. Chickpea flour's natural binding agents result in a crispy coating all around.

SERVES 4 TO 6

TANGY BASIL MAYO

½ cup (120 ml) Magic Mayo (page 151)

5 pepperoncini peppers

1 tablespoon pepperoncini pepper liquid from the jar

1 tablespoon olive oil

1 garlic clove, peeled, or ½ teaspoon Garlic Paste (page 163)

½ tightly packed cup (30 g) fresh basil leaves, plus more for garnish

1½ teaspoons maple syrup

1 teaspoon kosher salt

1 teaspoon paprika

FRIED GREEN TOMATOES

4 or 5 medium or large green (unripe) tomatoes

1 tablespoon kosher salt

¼ cup (25 g) chickpea flour

½ cup (120 ml) unsweetened plant-based milk

¾ cup (100 g) cornmeal

½ cup (65 g) cornstarch

¼ cup (30 g) all-purpose flour

1 teaspoon smoked sweet paprika

1 teaspoon ground cumin

½ teaspoon black pepper

½ teaspoon granulated sugar

2 cups (480 ml) neutral oil, for frying

Place the mayo, peppers, pepper liquid, oil, garlic, basil, maple syrup, salt, and paprika in a blender or food processor. Blend until smooth and light

(continued)

green in color. Transfer to a bowl, cover tightly with plastic wrap, and store in the fridge until you're ready to serve.

Cut the tomatoes into ½-inch-thick (1 cm) slices and lay them out on a baking sheet. Sprinkle with 1½ teaspoons of the kosher salt to draw out excess moisture. Let the tomatoes sit for at least 10 minutes.

Set up coating and dredging stations: Whisk the chickpea flour, milk, and the remaining 1½ teaspoons kosher salt in a medium bowl until no chickpea flour lumps remain. Combine the cornmeal, cornstarch, flour, paprika, cumin, pepper, and sugar in a shallow baking dish or pie dish and set it next to the batter. Place a baking sheet fitted with a wire rack next to the dredge mix. Top another wire rack with paper towels and place it near the stove.

Pat the tomato slices dry, then, one at a time, dip a tomato slice in the batter, coating it completely. Place it in the dredge and lightly press it with a clean hand; flip to coat both sides. Place the coated tomato slice on the wire rack on the baking sheet. Repeat with the remaining tomato slices. Place the coated tomatoes in the refrigerator to set while you heat the oil.

Pour oil into a 10-inch (25 cm) cast-iron skillet and set it over medium heat. Once the oil reaches 350°F (175°C) on a deep-fry thermometer, gently place 3 or 4 tomato slices into the oil. They should immediately begin to bubble and brown lightly. Fry for 2 minutes on each side, flipping once, or until they're deeply golden brown on both sides. Use a slotted spoon or spider to transfer the slices to the paper towel–lined wire rack. Let the oil return to 350°F (175°C) before repeating with more tomato slices. Serve the tomatoes hot with the basil mayo alongside.

Freestyle It

> Make the dipping sauce uniquely yours. You can swap in any tender herb, such as cilantro or parsley, for the basil. And if you don't keep jarred pepperoncini on hand, feel free to reach for any other pickled situation. A handful of drained capers, chopped dill pickles, or chopped pickled jalapeños will do the trick.

Creamy Labneh and Spiced Peach Dip

Upgrade your usual chip-and-dip spread with some inspiration from modern mezzes, with a touch of Southern flair. Labneh, a traditional Middle Eastern strained yogurt, is a simple vehicle for creamy dips. After straining plant-based yogurt overnight, you'll be left with a tart and savory base for any type of dip you please. Keep it simple or make it fancy: Fry some spices with a big dollop of store-bought peach jam to engineer an elegant appetizer or afternoon snack. Since the labneh takes at least one day to make, feel free to double the recipe and keep extra labneh in your fridge at all times to dollop onto a bowl of Tex-Mex Macaroni Soup (page 99) or spread under Southern-Style Tomato Toast (page 43).

SERVES 4 TO 6

LABNEH

2 cups (480 g) coconut yogurt

1 tablespoon olive oil

1½ teaspoons freshly squeezed lemon juice

1½ teaspoons kosher salt

SPICED PEACH SAUCE

2 tablespoons neutral oil

1 tablespoon cumin seeds

1½ teaspoons white sesame seeds

½ teaspoon red pepper flakes

½ teaspoon kosher salt

½ cup (175 g) peach jam

Cucumber slices, crackers, or fresh bread, for serving

Whisk together the coconut yogurt, oil, lemon juice, and salt in a medium mixing bowl until thoroughly combined. Taste for salt and acidity and adjust to your preference. Place a large fine-mesh sieve over a large bowl. Line the sieve with cheesecloth, a clean, thin kitchen towel, or two or three sheets of paper towels. Spoon the yogurt mixture into the sieve. Place a sheet of plastic wrap directly onto the surface of the yogurt. Press lightly on the yogurt to begin the water drainage. Tightly wrap the entire sieve-and-bowl arrangement in plastic wrap and place in the fridge. Let the yogurt

(continued)

drain for at least 8 and up to 24 hours, until it is almost as thick as cream cheese.

Once the labneh has finished draining, spoon it into a small serving bowl and refrigerate it until you're ready to serve.

Heat the oil in a small saucepan over medium heat. When the oil begins to shimmer, add the cumin seeds, sesame seeds, red pepper flakes, and salt. Stir vigorously for 2 minutes, or until the spices are fragrant. Add the peach jam and ¼ cup (60 ml) water and whisk to combine, ensuring no streaks of oil are visibly separate from the syrupy peach jam. Let the sauce come to a boil. When bubbles begin to rapidly form and pop in the center of the sauce, remove from the heat. Continue stirring for 2 minutes to release more steam and cool the sauce down.

Drizzle the warm sauce over the labneh. Use the back of a spoon to swirl the sauce into divots in the labneh, creating a swirl effect. Serve immediately with fresh cucumber slices, crackers, or fresh bread.

Crispy Golden Tofu

Freeze and thaw tofu in advance for the ultimate crispy, airy nuggets, but no sweat if you use a package straight from the fridge.

2 tablespoons olive oil

1 block (14 ounces/397 g) firm tofu, frozen and thawed

½ tablespoon kosher salt

1 tablespoon soy sauce

½ teaspoon black pepper

½ teaspoon granulated sugar

2 tablespoons cornstarch

3 tablespoons nutritional yeast

Steamed white rice, for serving (optional)

Copycat Sauce (page 153) or Maple Mustard BBQ Sauce (page 162), for serving

Preheat the oven to 400°F (205°C). Line a baking sheet with aluminum foil and drizzle with 1 tablespoon of the olive oil. Set aside.

Cut the tofu into 1-inch (2 cm) cubes, or tear it into craggy pieces by hand. Use paper towels to press the tofu pieces and absorb any excess water.

Toss the tofu cubes, salt, soy sauce, pepper, sugar, and the remaining 1 tablespoon olive oil in a large mixing bowl. Add the cornstarch and 1 tablespoon of the nutritional yeast and toss again to evenly distribute the dry ingredients. Spread out the tofu on the prepared baking sheet and bake for 25 minutes, or until the tofu is golden brown and crisp to the touch.

Transfer the tofu to a clean mixing bowl. Add the remaining 2 tablespoons nutritional yeast and a pinch of salt and toss to coat. Serve the tofu immediately with warm rice or on its own, with the sauce alongside.

Meal-ify It

› Or chop broccoli, cauliflower, and carrots, into 2-inch (5 cm) pieces and arrange on a baking sheet. Drizzle with olive oil and sprinkle with 2 teaspoons kosher salt, nutritional yeast, and black pepper. Bake at 450°F (232°C) for 35 minutes, until golden. Serve with the tofu.

A Tofu for Every Occasion

From creamy sauces to crispy crumbles, different types of tofu can be employed in dishes where you least expect it.

SOFT SILKEN TOFU

Think of this as a substitute for cream in sauces, dips, and desserts. Silken tofu in its original form has a pudding-like texture. It can be blended with any flavorful ingredients you wish to highlight. Use it to make the silken tofu chocolate pie filling on page 126 or as a substitute in traditionally mayo-based sauces (pages 151 and 153).

MEDIUM-FIRM, FIRM, AND EXTRA FIRM TOFU

These are the tofus you're probably most familiar with, and for good reason. They can be crumbled, sautéed, and fried to perfection. Whenever you buy a package of medium-firm or firm tofu, chuck it in your freezer for future use. Freezing firmer tofu gives it a textural makeover: The water pockets in the tofu expand when frozen, creating larger pores and a fluffier tofu once thawed. Bonus: When you freeze tofu, its larger pores and spongy texture make it much easier to press the water out when you're ready to cook it.

Easy Being Green Tomato and Honeydew Salad

In this verdant celebration of summer's best produce, green tomatoes and honeydew melon are tossed in a simple salad dressing made with ingredients you likely already have. If leafy salads typically bore you, take a stab at these greens covered in toasted coconut flakes. You may know coconut as the star of Southern-style coconut cake, but its nutty and tropical flavors are just as welcome in savory applications. Coconut flakes are the fragrant, nutty, fatty, and easy salad topping you've been looking for.

SERVES 4

½ medium honeydew melon

3 or 4 medium green (unripe) tomatoes

1 teaspoon kosher salt

½ packed cup (30 g) fresh parsley leaves

½ packed cup (30 g) fresh mint leaves

1 jalapeño pepper

¼ cup (60 ml) olive oil

¼ cup (60 ml) freshly squeezed lime juice

¼ cup (60 ml) maple syrup

½ cup (50 g) unsweetened coconut flakes

Use a metal spoon to scoop out the seeds from the melon. Peel the melon using a sharp knife, then cut it into ¼-inch-thick (6 mm) slices, about 1½ inches (3 cm) long. Slice the tomatoes crosswise into ¼-inch-thick (6 mm) slices. Place the tomato and honeydew slices in a large bowl and sprinkle with the salt. Chop the parsley and mint leaves.

Slice the jalapeño in half lengthwise; remove and discard the stem and seeds. Finely mince the jalapeño and transfer it to an 8-ounce (240 ml) glass jar. Add the olive oil, lime juice, and maple syrup; tightly twist the

(continued)

lid shut and vigorously shake the jar to emulsify the dressing. Add ¼ cup (60 ml) of the dressing to the tomatoes and melon and toss to combine. Taste for salt and adjust to your preference. Add the herbs and set aside in the fridge.

Place a large dry skillet over medium heat and add the coconut flakes. Allow the flakes to toast undisturbed for 2 minutes, or until the edges start to brown. Once lightly golden brown, stir the flakes for another 2 minutes, until all the flakes are golden brown.

Transfer the chilled salad to a serving dish and sprinkle with the toasted coconut and extra dressing, if desired. Serve immediately.

Freestyle It

> Use any acid or oil you like to make the dressing—just make sure to stick to the proportions listed in the recipe and taste as you go. Any green herbs would taste great in this salad, but the combination of mint and the toasted coconut flakes is sure to surprise your taste buds with a uniquely fragrant freshness.

Creamy Scallion-Potato Salad

This recipe combines my love for crispy golden potatoes and classic potato salad. The potatoes are baked (instead of boiled) alongside a handful of scallions that eventually get blitzed into the creamy mayo that holds this salad together. The sweet roasted scallions provide an extra boost of complexity in an already delectable miso- and tofu-based mayo. Since there are no animal products involved, this potato salad can stay out for a few hours at a potluck without spoiling.

SERVES 4

6 scallions, trimmed

1½ pounds (675 g) baby Yukon Gold potatoes

2 tablespoons olive oil

2 teaspoons kosher salt

1 package (16 ounces/450 g) soft silken tofu

2 tablespoons freshly squeezed lemon juice

1 tablespoon neutral oil

1 tablespoon white miso

1 tablespoon maple syrup

½ teaspoon red pepper flakes

Preheat the oven to 400°F (205°C). Line a large baking sheet with aluminum foil.

Place 4 of the scallions on one side of the prepared baking sheet. Thinly slice the remaining 2 scallions and set aside for garnish.

Wash and dry the potatoes. Cut the potatoes into 1-inch (2cm) pieces and add them to a large mixing bowl. Add the olive oil and 1 teaspoon of the salt and toss to coat. Spread out the potatoes alongside the scallions on the baking sheet. Set the mixing bowl aside (to save yourself from washing it twice!). Bake the potatoes and scallions for 30 minutes, flipping the potatoes with a spatula once halfway through baking. Remove from the oven when potatoes are a deep golden brown and the scallions are brown and withered.

(continued)

Using tongs, transfer the roasted scallions to a food processor or blender. Add the tofu, lemon juice, neutral oil, miso, maple syrup, the remaining teaspoon of salt, and red pepper flakes and blend for 1 to 2 minutes, until completely smooth. Taste for salt and acidity and adjust to your preference—if it tastes too salty or sour, add more oil or maple syrup.

Transfer the potatoes and ½ cup (120 ml) of the scallion sauce to the mixing bowl and toss to combine. Garnish with the reserved scallions and serve.

Store the potato salad in an airtight container in the refrigerator for up to 3 days. Store the remainder of the scallion sauce in an airtight container or tightly capped jar for up to 1 month. It's a great dipping sauce or condiment to have on hand.

Meal-ify It

> This recipe is begging to be made with chickpeas or baked tofu if you don't have potatoes on hand. In place of potatoes, use the same volume of canned chickpeas (strained and rinsed) and roast them in the oven at 400°F (205°C) for 10 minutes. That way, you can make it a filling and protein-packed meal. To substitute the potatoes with tofu, pat and dry a 14-ounce (397 g) package of firm tofu with paper towels or a kitchen towel. Slice the tofu into 1-inch (2 cm) cubes. Heat a nonstick skillet over medium-high heat and add 2 tablespoons of olive oil. After warming the oil for 2 to 3 minutes, add the tofu cubes in one layer. Fry the tofu on one side, undisturbed, for 5 to 7 minutes, or until the underside is golden brown. Flip the tofu cubes and fry on a second side for another 5 to 7 minutes, adding another tablespoon of olive oil if necessary. Once the tofu is mostly golden brown, remove it from the pan and let cool for 10 minutes before continuing the rest of the recipe. Add any other fresh greens or herbs in addition to the scallions when combining the sauce with the rest of the ingredients.

Dinners & Mains

Growing up in the South, you learn that you always expand a meal to feed as many people as want to join. While these recipes aren't exclusive to dinner parties or groups, it's safe to say a gooey scoop of either mac and cheese (pages 67 and 71) sure does taste better when shared with others. These family-style meals are ideal to make for yourself on a Saturday night in or the next time you gather your loved ones for dinner.

Mushroom and Potato Pot Pie Casserole

Don't let the idea of making a pot pie intimidate you. The only thing that makes this dish a pie is the fact that a sheet of puff pastry bakes on top of its rich and hearty filling. This recipe is especially quick if you already have a batch of Silky Cashew Cream (page 158) in your freezer or fridge.

SERVES 4 OR 5

2 medium potatoes (about 1 pound/450 g), peeled

2 large carrots (about 2 ounces/55 g), peeled

1 large onion, peeled

3 large celery stalks

8 ounces (225 g) cremini or portobello mushrooms

3 tablespoons olive oil

4 garlic cloves, peeled and minced, or 2 teaspoons Garlic Paste (page 163)

1 tablespoon white miso

1 cup (240 ml) vegetable broth

1 cup (240 g) Silky Cashew Cream (page 158)

1 teaspoon dried thyme

1 pinch ground nutmeg

1 tablespoon kosher salt

1 teaspoon black pepper

All-purpose flour

1 sheet vegan puff pastry, thawed according to package instructions

1 tablespoon unsweetened oat milk, for brushing

Preheat the oven to the temperature recommended on the puff pastry package.

Dice the potatoes, carrots, and onion into 1-inch (2 cm) pieces. Cut off and discard the wide white end of the celery and dice the stalks and leafy ends into 1-inch (2 cm) pieces. Wipe the mushrooms clean with a paper towel and cut into ½-inch-thick (1 cm) slices. Set aside the onion and celery in one batch, the potatoes and carrots together in another, and mushrooms separately.

Pour the olive oil into a large high-sided skillet set over medium heat. Add the onion and celery. Cook for 3 to 4 minutes, until softened. Add the garlic, miso, and mushrooms to the skillet and cook for another 5 minutes,

(continued)

stirring occasionally, until the mushrooms have softened and the miso and garlic begin to brown with the mushrooms. Add the potatoes and carrots and cook for 5 minutes, or until they soften slightly.

Whisk the vegetable broth, cashew cream, thyme, nutmeg, salt, and pepper in a large mixing bowl until well combined. Pour this into the skillet. Stir everything together and bring to a simmer. Cook for 10 to 15 minutes, stirring occasionally, until the sauce thickens and all the vegetables are tender. Taste for salt and adjust the seasonings to your preference. Transfer the filling to a 9-inch (23 cm) pie dish. Place the pie dish in the fridge to cool as much as possible while you prepare the pastry.

On a lightly floured surface, roll out the puff pastry sheet to a 10 × 10-inch (25 × 25 cm) square.

Place the puff pastry over the pie dish, covering the filling completely. Use a fork to press down and seal the edges of the pastry on the edge of the pie dish. Brush the puff pastry with the oat milk for a golden and lacquered finish. Cut 5 small slits in the center of the pastry to allow steam to escape during baking.

Bake for 20 to 25 minutes, until the puff pastry is golden brown and crispy. Let the pie cool for 10 minutes before serving.

Freestyle It

> If the listed vegetables aren't the pot pie fillings of your dreams, you can get creative with any hearty produce you desire. Sweet potatoes, green beans, broccoli—even beans—are all fair game in this versatile recipe. Just be sure to cut the vegetables to 1-inch (2 cm) pieces, enough to total 5 cups (725 g).

(Fancy) French Onion Mac and Cheese

There are limitless possibilities for making a creamy sauce and conveniently small pasta taste good, but what makes a mac and cheese *great* is texture and depth of flavor. This fancy-ish, French onion soup–inspired take on mac and cheese accomplishes both with deeply browned onions and a crispy crouton topping. This mac and cheese rides on umami from the caramelized onions and veggie broth and gets its creaminess from Silky Cashew Cream (page 158). For a classic Southern version of mac and cheese, turn to page 71.

SERVES 4 TO 6

FRENCH ONION TOPPING

3 tablespoons olive oil, plus more for greasing the baking dish

½ loaf French baguette or country bread (about 4 ounces/115 g)

1 cup (55 g) store-bought fried onions

½ teaspoon kosher salt

MAC AND CHEESE

3 large onions, peeled

2 tablespoons olive oil

1 pound (454 g) elbow macaroni or small shells

4 garlic cloves, peeled, or 2 teaspoons Garlic Paste (page 163)

2 tablespoons soy sauce

1 tablespoon balsamic vinegar

1 tablespoon brown sugar

2 cups (480 g) Silky Cashew Cream (page 158)

1 cup (240 ml) vegetable broth, plus more if needed

½ cup (40 g) nutritional yeast

1 teaspoon dried thyme

1 tablespoon kosher salt

1 teaspoon black pepper

Preheat the oven to 375°F (190°C). Grease a 13 × 9-inch (33 × 23 cm) baking dish with a little olive oil.

Tear the bread into roughly 1-inch (2 cm) pieces. Combine the bread pieces and fried onions in a large mixing bowl and drizzle with the olive oil and salt. Toss to combine. Set aside.

(continued)

Thinly slice the onions. Add the onions and olive oil to a large heavy-bottomed pot or Dutch oven and set the pot over medium-low heat. Stir the onions with a silicone spatula or wooden spoon occasionally while they caramelize for at least 15 or 20 minutes, until they have shrunk and turned a deep golden brown.

While the onions caramelize, bring a large pot of water to a boil, salt it, and cook the macaroni according to the package instructions. Drain and set aside.

Mince the garlic cloves, if using. Add the garlic to the caramelized onions and fry until fragrant and mixed in, about 3 minutes. Add the soy sauce, balsamic vinegar, and brown sugar. Cook for another 2 minutes, allowing the flavors to meld.

Increase the heat to medium-high. Stir in the cashew cream, vegetable broth, nutritional yeast, dried thyme, salt, and pepper until well combined.

Continue stirring occasionally while the sauce simmers and thickens. If the sauce seems too thick, add more vegetable broth 1 tablespoon at a time. Taste for salt and adjust to your preference. The sauce should have a looser, gravy-like consistency since it will thicken further once mixed with the macaroni.

Remove the pot from heat and add the cooked macaroni. Stir to coat the macaroni evenly with the sauce. Transfer the mac and cheese mixture to the greased baking dish. Sprinkle the French onion topping evenly on top. Cover the baking dish with foil and bake for 10 minutes.

Remove the foil and bake for another 5 to 10 minutes, until the cheese has melted and the topping is crispy and golden. Let the mac and cheese cool for 5 minutes before serving.

(Classic) Cracker-Crusted Mac and Cheese

No less delicious than its "fancy" counterpart, this more traditional take on the classic casserole celebrates the nostalgic, golden, cheesy pasta you grew up eating on Thanksgiving and at potlucks. The golden-brown Ritz Cracker topping (yes, it's vegan!) ties everything together just like you remember.

SERVES 4 TO 6

2 tablespoons (30 g) plant-based butter, plus more for the baking dish

About 55 (180 g) Ritz Crackers

1 pound (454 g) elbow macaroni or small shells

2 cups (480 g) Silky Cashew Cream (page 158)

1 cup (240 ml) vegetable broth

¼ cup (40 g) nutritional yeast

2 tablespoons freshly squeezed lemon juice

1 tablespoon soy sauce

1 tablespoon white miso

½ teaspoon garlic powder

½ teaspoon onion powder

¼ teaspoon ground turmeric

1 tablespoon kosher salt

1 teaspoon black pepper

Preheat the oven to 375°F (190°C). Lightly grease a 13 × 9-inch (33 × 23 cm) baking dish with butter.

Put the crackers in a large resealable bag and seal it shut, making sure to release any excess air from the bag. Loosely wrap a kitchen towel around the bag, place it on the counter, and beat with a large bottle, rolling pin, or heavy can to crush the crackers. Melt the butter and pour it into the bag. Seal the bag again and shake or squeeze it to distribute the butter to all the cracker crumbs.

Cook the macaroni for 1 minute less than advised on the package instructions. Set a colander in a large heatproof bowl in the sink. Drain the

(continued)

macaroni, reserving 1 cup (240 ml) of the cooking water and discarding the rest. Return the macaroni to the pot along with the reserved cooking water.

In a large mixing bowl, combine the cashew cream, vegetable broth, nutritional yeast, lemon juice, soy sauce, miso, garlic powder, onion powder, turmeric, salt, and pepper. Mix well until smooth, making sure no clumps of miso remain.

Pour the sauce over the macaroni and set the pot over medium heat. Stir to combine and coat the macaroni with sauce and simmer for about 10 minutes, until the sauce thickens. Taste for salt and adjust to your preference.

When the sauce is still slightly loose, transfer the mixture to the greased baking dish. Sprinkle the cracker topping over the top and lightly pat into the surface. Bake for 20 minutes, or until the top is golden and crispy. Let cool for 5 minutes before serving.

Pimento Cheese Pasta

Pimento cheese, a beloved Southern delicacy, is a creamy and tangy spread or dip made from grated sharp cheddar cheese and diced pimiento peppers. This pasta dish re-creates its bold and cheesy flavors with a combination of miso, peppers, and my favorite creamy pasta sauce base, silken tofu. This recipe makes enough sauce for two batches of pasta, so you can freeze half of it and save it for a quick weeknight meal in the future.

SERVES 3 OR 4

Salt

10 ounces (285 g) small shells or penne

1 red bell pepper

1 large or 2 small celery stalks

1 large yellow onion, peeled

3 tablespoons extra virgin olive oil

1 tablespoon white miso

½ teaspoon ground turmeric

½ teaspoon smoked sweet paprika

½ teaspoon paprika

1 package (16 ounces/450 g) soft silken tofu

1 cup (150 g) drained store-bought roasted red peppers or pimiento peppers

2 tablespoons freshly squeezed lemon juice

1 tablespoon Garlic Paste (page 163) or 6 garlic cloves, peeled

1 tablespoon nutritional yeast

1 teaspoon red pepper flakes

Salt

3 scallions, trimmed and thinly sliced

Fill a large pot with 4 quarts (4 L) water and add about 4 tablespoons kosher salt. Set over high heat and bring to a boil. Once the water is vigorously boiling, add the pasta and cook until al dente, according to package directions.

While the pasta cooks, cut the bell pepper in half lengthwise. Cut out and discard the stem, seedy core, and white ribs. Dice the bell pepper into ¼-inch (6 mm) pieces. Cut off and discard the wide white end of the celery. Slice the stalks in half lengthwise then cut crosswise into ¼-inch (6 mm) pieces. Dice the onion into ¼-inch (6 mm) pieces.

(continued)

Add the olive oil, bell pepper, onion, and celery to a large high-sided skillet or pot set over medium heat. Cook and stir with a silicone spatula or wooden spoon for 5 minutes, or until the vegetables have softened. Reduce the heat to low and add the miso, turmeric, smoked sweet paprika, and regular paprika. Continue stirring with the spatula to break down the miso. Add a tablespoon water if needed to help dissolve the miso. Simmer on low heat for another 5 minutes.

When the pasta is al dente, set a colander in a large heatproof bowl in the sink. Drain the pasta, reserving 2 cups (480 ml) of the cooking water and discarding the rest. Set the pasta aside.

Add the tofu, roasted peppers, lemon juice, garlic, nutritional yeast, and red pepper flakes to a blender and blend until smooth, about 2 minutes. Set aside half of the sauce in an airtight container or tightly capped jar.

Add the drained pasta to the skillet with the cooked vegetables. Add the remaining half of the sauce and 1 cup (240 ml) of the pasta cooking water. Toss or stir everything together over medium-low heat for 4 to 5 minutes, until the water has been absorbed into the pasta and the glossy sauce clings to the pasta. Add extra pasta cooking water a few tablespoons at a time, if the sauce is thicker than you'd like. (Keep in mind that adding more pasta water will loosen it but also add saltiness.) Taste the sauce and add more salt if necessary.

Garnish the pasta with the scallions and serve immediately.

A Vegan's Fried Chicken Sandwich Special

Nothing screams THE SOUTH more than a subtly sweet and outrageously crisp golden fried chicken—or in this case, mushroom—sandwich. Clusters of oyster mushrooms create a meaty, chicken-like texture that holds its own in this sandwich, leaving nothing to be desired. Pair the sandwich with sweet pickles, fresh tomatoes, and a slathering of Copycat Sauce (page 153) for the ultimate deluxe experience.

MAKES 4 SANDWICHES

MARINATED MUSHROOMS

¾ cup (80 ml) unsweetened plant-based milk

½ cup (120 ml) pickle juice (from a jar)

¼ cup (60 ml) hot sauce

3 tablespoons brown sugar

½ teaspoon paprika

½ teaspoon garlic powder

½ teaspoon onion powder

½ teaspoon kosher salt

¼ teaspoon black pepper

8 ounces (225 g) large oyster mushrooms

DREDGE

1 cup (125 g) all-purpose flour

½ cup (65 g) cornstarch

2 teaspoons paprika

1 teaspoon garlic powder

1 teaspoon onion powder

1 teaspoon kosher salt

½ teaspoon black pepper

SANDWICH

Neutral oil, for frying

4 plant-based burger buns

Pickle slices

Lettuce leaves

Tomato slices

Magic Mayo (page 151) or Copycat Sauce (page 153)

Whisk together the milk, pickle juice, hot sauce, brown sugar, paprika, garlic powder, onion powder, salt, and pepper in a large mixing bowl.

Divide the oyster mushrooms into 4 large, sandwich-size portions. Place the mushrooms in a gallon-size (4 L) resealable bag, then place the bag in

(continued)

a wide, shallow bowl. Pour the marinade over the mushrooms, ensuring they are well coated. Press excess air out of the bag and seal it. Marinate the mushrooms in the refrigerator for at least 30 minutes, or up to overnight.

When you're ready to make the sandwiches, remove the mushrooms from the fridge and carefully pour out as much of the marinade as possible.

Whisk together the flour, cornstarch, paprika, garlic powder, onion powder, salt, and pepper in a small bowl. Transfer the dredge to the bag of mushrooms and shake to evenly distribute it and coat the mushrooms. Be gentle while shaking, so as to not break up the mushroom portions. Shaking off any excess dredge, carefully transfer the mushrooms to a wire rack placed over a baking sheet. Refrigerate the mushrooms while the oil heats.

Fill a large heavy-bottomed pot with 3 to 4 inches (8 to 10 cm) of oil. Set the pot over medium heat. Use a deep-fry thermometer to check the temperature of the oil, adjusting the heat to maintain it at 350°F (175°C). Set a paper towel–topped wire rack near the stove for the cooked mushrooms.

Use a slotted spoon or spider to carefully transfer 1 or 2 mushroom portions to the oil. Fry on each side until golden brown, flipping once, about 3 minutes per side. Keep the mushrooms moving around in the oil to ensure an even color across the mushrooms. When golden brown, use the slotted spoon to transfer the mushrooms to the paper towel–covered wire rack to drain and cool. Fry and drain the remaining mushroom patties. Warm the buns cut side down in a dry skillet for 5 minutes over medium heat, until just crispy.

Arrange the pickles, lettuce, and tomatoes on a platter for your guests to take from as they prefer. Spread mayo on the buns and top each with a mushroom patty. Allow your guests to assemble their sandwiches as they prefer.

Freestyle It

> In the mood for nuggets instead of a sandwich? Follow the recipe, but tear the mushrooms into smaller pieces and use the same sauce for dipping.
> These mushroom patties also taste great slathered with maple syrup and sandwiched within Flaky Biscuits (page 23).

Fried Food 101

Deep-frying will not be intimidating when you keep these frying commandments in mind.

Set up a dredging station first: Set up two shallow pans, one with the dry ingredients and the other with wet ingredients. Use separate hands for dipping into the dry versus the wet. Whichever method you use, fit a wire rack over a baking sheet and place each dredged piece on the rack.

Dredge all the food to fry beforehand: This will facilitate a lower-stress frying environment. Place the dredged ingredients on a wire rack and refrigerate them while the frying oil heats, up to 15 minutes before frying. This will help the dredge bind to the surface of the food.

Keep extra frying oil nearby: Maintaining the heat of the oil is arguably the most finicky aspect of frying consistently golden-brown foods that are neither burnt nor raw. If you notice the food browning faster than directions indicate, the oil may be too hot. To cool down the frying oil, add more oil, about ½ cup (120 ml) at a time, and reduce the heat.

Use a paper towel–lined wire rack to drain and rest fried foods: Instead of placing fried food on paper towels on a plate or on a naked wire rack, line a rack with paper towels. The paper towels absorb excess oil, and the rack provides airflow, preventing the food from steaming and adding moisture to its crispy exterior.

Summer Squash Casserole

When your garden (or grocery store) is bustling with zucchini and yellow squash and you've brought home more of it than you know what to do with, this recipe will give you a good reason to cook them in bulk. Celebrate the humble summer squash in a not-too-rich casserole studded with juicy tomatoes and fresh basil, and topped with a generous layer of crispy panko breadcrumbs.

SERVES 4 TO 6

2 pounds (900 g) summer squash or zucchini

1 cup (150 g) cherry tomatoes

1 large onion, peeled

¼ cup (60 ml) olive oil

2 garlic cloves, peeled, or 1 teaspoon Garlic Paste (page 163)

4 teaspoons kosher salt

2 tablespoons sliced pickled jalapeños

1 cup (240 g) Silky Cashew Cream (page 158)

1 packed cup (60 g) fresh basil leaves, plus more for garnish

1 cup (100 g) vegan panko breadcrumbs

¼ cup (40 g) nutritional yeast

¼ teaspoon dried oregano

1 teaspoon black pepper

Preheat the oven to 375°F (190°C).

Trim the ends off the squash and slice the squash into ¼-inch-thick (6 mm) rounds. Slice the cherry tomatoes in half. Dice the onion into ½-inch (1 cm) pieces. Set aside each vegetable separately.

Heat 1 tablespoon of the olive oil in a large straight-sided skillet over medium-low heat. Add the onion. Use a Microplane to grate the garlic cloves directly into the skillet, or add the garlic paste. Sauté until the onions become translucent and the garlic is fragrant, 3 to 4 minutes.

(continued)

Add the tomatoes, 1 teaspoon of salt, and pickled jalapeños and continue to cook for 5 to 6 minutes, until the tomatoes are just softened but not deflated. Transfer the vegetables to an 8 × 8-inch (20 × 20 cm) baking dish.

Wipe the skillet clean with a paper towel and pour in another tablespoon of the olive oil. Set the skillet over high heat. Once the oil begins to shimmer and smoke, add the squash, trying to keep it to one layer, and let it sit undisturbed for about 2 minutes. After the squash looks lightly charred on the underside, shake the pan, moving other squash slices to make contact with the skillet. Continue cooking on high heat for 2 minutes at a time, until most of the squash is lightly charred.

Transfer the charred squash to the baking dish. Add the cashew cream and 2 teaspoons salt. Tear half of the basil leaves into small pieces and sprinkle over the top. Stir everything together until totally combined.

Combine the breadcrumbs, the remaining 2 tablespoons olive oil, the nutritional yeast, dried oregano, 1 teaspoon salt, and the pepper in a small bowl. Sprinkle the breadcrumb mixture over the squash.

Bake for 20 to 25 minutes, until the casserole is bubbly and the breadcrumb topping has turned golden brown. Let cool for a few minutes before sprinkling with more freshly torn basil. Serve warm.

Casserole Culture

Casseroles represent the comfort, resourcefulness, and innovation in Southern cooking. These one-dish wonders are rooted deep in the region's Native American heritage. Some Cherokee and Choctaw people were known to create communal dishes by combining local crops like beans, corn, and squash, and slow-cooking them in large clay pots buried in the ground—a method that is reminiscent of modern casserole cooking.

The concept of casseroles as we know them today gained prominence in the South during the nineteenth century. As Southern families navigated the challenges of war, economic hardships, and limited resources, casseroles emerged as a practical solution, allowing cooks to stretch ingredients to feed large gatherings and supplying sustenance over the course of days.

From the early twentieth century onward, the rise of convenience foods, canned goods, and frozen ingredients provided new possibilities for cooks. Southern cooks utilized casseroles as a way to incorporate these now accessible ingredients into traditional Southern cooking, resulting in dishes like tuna noodle casserole and green bean casserole. Soon, casseroles would become the most convenient way to cook and share for groups of loved ones.

Church suppers, potlucks, and family gatherings further solidified the role of casseroles in Southern culture. These communal events often featured an array of casseroles, where each dish represented a family's favorite flavors and unique traditions. The practice of sharing casseroles also mirrored the strong sense of community and interconnectedness that make up the core tenets of Southern food culture.

Treat your own casseroles as an amalgam of comforts in a baking dish. No matter what a recipe calls for, what's in your fridge or what your local market has available is far more important. Pro tip: Double check the usual cook time for any vegetable you want to substitute into a casserole recipe. For example, root vegetables like turnips and carrots take much more time to cook through than summer squash, so make sure to adjust the cooking time to account for the difference.

Green Bean Casserole

This casserole can be polarizing: a beloved holiday food for some and an undesirably heavy side for others. But this version is light enough to make it the bulk of your dinner even when it's not Thanksgiving. My tastiest recipes are often the ones that are different shades of golden brown, ranging in texture from creamy to crispy—which is exactly what a crispy-onion crusted green bean casserole should be. Plus, the cashew cream will leave you feeling less weighed down, and ready for seconds . . . or thirds.

SERVES 6 TO 8

1 pound (450 g) fresh green beans

8 ounces (225 g) cremini or portobello mushrooms

1 large onion, peeled

2 tablespoons (30 g) plant-based butter

2 garlic cloves, peeled, or 1 teaspoon Garlic Paste (page 163)

2 cups (480 g) Silky Cashew Cream (page 158)

1 tablespoon white miso

½ teaspoon onion powder

½ teaspoon garlic powder

½ teaspoon dried thyme

1 to 2 pinches ground nutmeg

3 teaspoons kosher salt

1 teaspoon black pepper

1½ cups (165 g) store-bought fried onions

Preheat the oven to 375°F (190°C).

Slice the ends off the green beans. Wipe the mushrooms clean with a paper towel and slice them into ¼-inch-thick (6 mm) pieces. Dice the onion into ¼-inch (6 mm) half-moons.

Bring a large pot of water to a boil. Add the green beans and cook for 5 to 6 minutes, until they are crisp-tender. Drain the beans and set aside.

Melt the butter in a large skillet over medium heat. Add the onion and mushrooms. Sauté until the mushrooms have released their moisture and become golden brown, 8 to 10 minutes. Use a Microplane to grate the garlic cloves directly into the skillet, or add the garlic paste. Cook for another 1 minute, until fragrant.

Reduce the heat to low and add the cashew cream, miso, onion powder, garlic powder, thyme, nutmeg, salt, and pepper. Stir to combine, until the miso is completely incorporated into the sauce. Add the green beans and mix well, ensuring the beans are coated with the sauce. Simmer on low heat for 3 to 5 minutes, until the sauce is thick like a gravy and the green beans are still snappy when broken. Transfer the green bean mixture to an 8 × 8-inch (20 × 20 cm) baking dish.

Sprinkle the fried onions evenly over the top. Bake for 15 to 20 minutes, until the casserole is hot and bubbly and the onion topping has turned a deep golden brown. Let cool for at least 5 minutes before serving.

BBQ Eggplant and Slaw Sandwiches

Meat substitutes are handy, but they're not always necessary to satisfy your cravings for a meaty-tasting meal. Rely on eggplant's juicy yet meaty texture and ability to absorb a sticky barbecue sauce in this plant-based take on a brisket sandwich.

SERVES 4

SLAW

1 cup (50 g) store-bought coleslaw mix

1 cup (100 g) store-bought shredded carrots

3 tablespoons chopped pickled jalapeños, plus 2 tablespoons pickling liquid

1 tablespoon maple syrup

1 teaspoon Dijon mustard

1 teaspoon kosher salt

BBQ EGGPLANT

8 large Chinese eggplants (about 4 pounds/2 kg total)

2 tablespoons kosher salt

¼ cup (30 g) cornstarch

¼ cup (60 ml) olive oil

SANDWICHES

8 slices Texas toast or rye bread

1 cup (240 ml) Maple Mustard BBQ Sauce (page 162)

Add the coleslaw mix, carrots, pickled jalapeños, pickling liquid, maple syrup, mustard, and salt to a large mixing bowl. Stir until the liquids are completely combined and have coated the vegetables. Set aside in the refrigerator for the flavors to meld until it's time to assemble the sandwiches.

Carefully slice the skin off each eggplant, making sure to not cut off too much of the flesh.

Slice the ends off the eggplants, then cut each eggplant lengthwise in half. Cut these pieces in half crosswise, leaving you with four planks per eggplant.

Arrange the eggplant planks on a paper towel–lined baking sheet or large platter and sprinkle with the salt to draw out excess moisture.

(continued)

Let sit for about 10 minutes. Pat dry with another paper towel or a clean kitchen towel. Transfer the eggplant planks to a large mixing bowl and sprinkle with the cornstarch. Toss together to evenly coat the eggplant. Set aside.

Add 2 tablespoons of the olive oil to a large nonstick skillet and set it over medium heat. When the oil is hot and shimmering, place as many eggplant planks as possible in the skillet without overlapping. Increase the heat to medium-high and fry the eggplant for 2 to 3 minutes on each side, until golden brown and lightly crisped. Transfer the fried eggplant to a paper towel–lined plate or wire rack. Repeat with the remaining olive oil and eggplant planks. Allow the eggplant to cool for at least 10 minutes before assembling the sandwiches.

While the eggplant cools, toast the bread.

Brush a generous amount of the barbecue sauce on both sides of the eggplant planks. Pile the eggplant onto half the slices of bread. Scoop a large serving of slaw on top of the eggplant and finish with the top slice of bread. Slice into triangles and serve immediately.

Soups & Stews

Soups may be humble in their preparation, but can be elevated with minor adjustments every step of the way. Indulge in a luscious chickpea broth, cheesy broccoli soup, or hearty kale porridge. Each recipe includes ideas for toppings and crunchies that will make even the homiest cup of soup taste a little fancy.

Creamy Chickpea Noodle Soup

You can achieve a velvety soup without a single dairy ingredient. Chickpeas and chickpea flour join forces to brew a rich and creamy broth that will heal you on your sick days and impress your taste buds with its deep, savory flavors anytime.

SERVES 4 TO 6

1 medium onion, peeled

2 tablespoons olive oil

3 garlic cloves, peeled

1-inch (2 cm) piece fresh ginger, peeled

2 medium carrots, peeled

3 celery stalks

1 cup (90 g) chickpea flour

1 tablespoon kosher salt

½ teaspoon black pepper

½ teaspoon ground cumin

½ teaspoon ground turmeric

1 carton (32 ounces/907 g) low-sodium vegetable broth

1 can (15 ounces/425 g) chickpeas, rinsed and drained

4 cups (960 ml) unsweetened soy or oat milk

10 ounces (285 g) spaghetti or bucatini

1 teaspoon dried thyme

½ teaspoon dried rosemary

Chopped fresh cilantro, for garnish

Lemon wedges, for serving

Dice the onion into ½-inch (1 cm) pieces. Add it to a large pot with the olive oil. Mince the garlic and ginger and set aside. Slice the carrots into ¼-inch-thick (6 mm) rounds. Cut off and discard the wide white ends of the celery and dice the stalks and leafy ends into ½-inch (1 cm) pieces.

Set the pot with the onions over medium heat and sauté the onions for 2 to 3 minutes, until just translucent. Add the garlic, ginger, carrots, and celery and cook for another 4 to 5 minutes, stirring occasionally, until the carrots begin to soften.

Sprinkle the chickpea flour, salt, pepper, cumin, and turmeric over the vegetables and stir well to coat them evenly. Cook for 1 to 2 minutes,

(continued)

allowing the flour and spices to lightly toast. Slowly pour in the vegetable broth, whisking constantly to prevent lumps.

Add the chickpeas, soy milk, spaghetti, thyme, rosemary, and 1 cup (240 ml) water. Stir well to combine.

Bring the soup to a boil over high heat. Reduce the heat to medium and let the soup simmer, uncovered, for 20 to 25 minutes, until the chickpeas are soft enough to mash between your fingers. If you prefer a thinner broth, add more water or milk to adjust the consistency. Taste and adjust the seasoning with salt and pepper to your preference.

Serve the soup hot, garnished with cilantro and a squeeze of lemon juice.

Chickpea Flour Power

Chickpea has been used to thicken soups and stews, like the popular South Asian dish kadhi, for centuries. Known for its unique texture and binding properties, chickpea flour, also called gram flour or besan, imparts a luscious viscosity to soups that one would normally attempt to achieve with dairy products.

The magic of chickpea flour as a thickening agent lies in its composition. Derived from ground chickpeas, the flour contains soluble fiber and proteins that act as natural thickeners when combined with liquids. When added to a soup or stew, chickpea flour creates a smooth and silky consistency, enhancing the overall mouthfeel of the dish.

In order to achieve that velvety smoothness in other dishes, make a slurry of 2 parts chickpea flour and 1 part water or other liquid and whisk until smooth. Add the slurry to a simmering soup or stew while continuously stirring. As the mixture heats up, the proteins and starches present in the chickpea flour begin to activate, causing the liquid to thicken. The result is a creamy, cohesive consistency that elevates the overall dining experience.

Aside from its thickening capabilities, chickpea flour also imparts a unique nutty, earthy flavor to dishes. It harmonizes beautifully with the cheesy flavor of nutritional yeast, making it an ideal component of the Cheesy Broccoli Soup (page 97).

When incorporating chickpea flour into soups and stews, it's important to follow a few key steps to achieve the desired results. First, sift the chickpea flour to remove any clumps, guaranteeing a smooth consistency in the final dish. Second, when using the slurry, take care to add it to the hot liquid gradually while stirring constantly. This prevents lumps from forming and ensures even distribution of the chickpea flour throughout the soup.

Chickpea flour's ability to thicken soups offers a culinary advantage for those seeking plant-based or gluten-free alternatives to conventional thickeners. As the culinary world embraces diverse ingredients, chickpea flour stands as a versatile tool that caters to a range of needs without compromising taste or quality.

Cheesy Broccoli Soup with Pesto Croutons

There are not many fast-food chains known for their soup, especially not a broccoli soup, but this recipe is an homage to Panera's famous broccoli cheddar soup. To replace the bread bowl they serve their soup in, you'll make an arguably tastier (and more functional) batch of pesto-basted croutons that you can throw together in 5 minutes while the soup simmers.

SERVES 4 TO 6

PESTO CROUTONS

4 or 5 slices bread (such as white bread, sourdough or half a French baguette)

2 tablespoons olive oil

2 tablespoons Any-Green Pesto (page 154)

1 teaspoon kosher salt

SOUP

1 large onion, peeled

1 tablespoon olive oil

2 garlic cloves, peeled

4 cups (400 g) broccoli florets (from 2 heads)

1 carton (32 ounces/907 g) vegetable broth

1 cup (240 g) Silky Cashew Cream (page 158)

½ cup (120 ml) unsweetened plant-based milk

¼ cup (40 g) nutritional yeast

1 teaspoon onion powder

1 teaspoon garlic powder

½ teaspoon smoked sweet paprika

Salt and pepper

Preheat the oven to 325°F (165°C).

Tear the bread into 1- to 2-inch (2 to 5 cm) pieces and add them to a large mixing bowl. Add the olive oil, pesto, and salt and toss to evenly coat the bread. Spread the bread in a single layer on a baking sheet. Bake for 15 to 20 minutes, until the croutons are golden and crispy. Set aside to cool.

Dice the onion into ½-inch (1 cm) pieces. Add the onion and olive oil to a large pot and set it over low heat.

(continued)

While the onions soften, thinly slice the garlic and chop the broccoli florets into 1-inch (2 cm) pieces. Add the garlic to the onions and sauté for 2 minutes, or until fragrant. Add the broccoli, increase the heat to medium-high, and sauté for 5 minutes, until the edges of the florets have lightly browned.

Add the vegetable broth and cashew cream and bring the soup to a boil, then reduce the heat to a simmer. Cook for 10 to 15 minutes, until the broccoli is tender when pierced with a fork or knife.

Use an immersion blender to puree the soup in the pot until it is mostly creamy, with some visible pieces of broccoli remaining. Or transfer the soup to a regular blender, working in batches if necessary, and return all the soup to the pot. Bring the soup to a simmer again over low heat. Stir in the milk, nutritional yeast, onion powder, garlic powder, smoked sweet paprika, and salt and pepper to taste. Simmer for 5 minutes, until the flavors meld.

Serve warm with the pesto croutons on top.

Tex-Mex Macaroni Soup

One-pot meals are a hack for both easy cooking and easy nutrition. This soup plays with the flavors and components of a Tex-Mex chili, but with a looser broth and pasta built into the soup. It wouldn't be far off to call this dish an ode to Hamburger Helper and SpaghettiOs.

SERVES 4 TO 6

1 large onion, peeled

1 tablespoon olive oil

2 bell peppers (any color)

2 canned chipotle peppers in adobo, wiped clean

1 tablespoon kosher salt

4 garlic cloves, peeled, or 2 teaspoons Garlic Paste (page 163)

1 can (14 ounces/400 g) diced tomatoes, with their juice

1 can (15 ounces/425 g) black beans, rinsed and drained

1 can (15 ounces/425 g) pinto beans, rinsed and drained

1 can (15 ounces/425 g) tomato sauce

1 cup (170 g) frozen corn kernels

1 teaspoon ground cumin

1 teaspoon smoked sweet paprika

1 teaspoon dried oregano

1 carton (32 ounces/907 g) vegetable broth

10 ounces (285 g) elbow macaroni or other small pasta shape

Chopped fresh cilantro, for garnish

Avocado slices, for garnish

Dice the onion into ½-inch (1 cm) pieces. Add it to a large pot along with the olive oil. Set the pot over low heat. Cook for 5 minutes, stirring occasionally, until translucent.

Cut the bell peppers in half lengthwise. Cut out and discard the stems, seedy cores, and white ribs. Dice the bell peppers into 1-inch ((2 cm) pieces. Mince the chipotle peppers.

Add the bell peppers, chipotle peppers, and salt to the onions. Use a Microplane to grate the garlic cloves directly into the pot, or add the

(continued)

garlic paste. Cook over medium heat for 5 to 7 minutes, until the peppers have softened.

Add the tomatoes and their juice, the black beans, pinto beans, tomato sauce, corn, cumin, paprika, and oregano. Stir well to combine for 5 minutes, scraping the bottom of the pot to prevent any spices from burning.

Add the vegetable broth and bring to a boil. Reduce the heat to low. Let the soup simmer, uncovered, for 10 minutes to allow the flavors to meld and the soup to thicken slightly.

Stir in the macaroni. Cover the pot, leaving the lid slightly ajar to let steam escape, and simmer for another 10 to 12 minutes, stirring occasionally, until the macaroni is cooked al dente. Remove from the heat and let the soup sit for a few minutes to thicken.

Serve the soup in bowls, garnished with cilantro and avocado.

Keep It Crunchy

Soups are inherently soft and soothing to eat. A warm bowl of noodle soup feels therapeutic while nourishing your belly at the same time. The addition of a crunchy element like croutons, garlic chips, or fried seeds brings a multidimensional sensory experience to soup that enhances both the taste and textural nuance of every spoonful. Most crunchy toppings can be thrown together on the stovetop or in the oven while your soup simmers, so why not get scrappy with some ingredients you already have and add a much-welcome crunch to your soups? In addition to homemade croutons (page 97) and garlic chips (page 113), here are other ways to add a pop of texture to soups and stews:

Toasted Nuts and Seeds: Toasted almonds, cashews, pumpkin seeds, or sunflower seeds provide a satisfying crunch. Dry-toast them in a skillet with a touch of salt, brown sugar, and smoked sweet paprika until they turn golden and fragrant.

Crispy Chickpeas: Roasted chickpeas are a protein-packed topping that adds a delightful crunch. Thoroughly drain cooked or canned chickpeas. Drizzle them with 1 tablespoon of olive oil and season them with your favorite spices, like paprika, cumin, or chili powder before roasting at 350°F (175°C) for 15 minutes.

Fried Onions: A tasty, crunchy, oniony topping that pairs well with many soups. Toss thinly sliced onions in all-purpose or chickpea flour to coat, then fry in neutral oil in a cast-iron skillet for 5 minutes, or until crispy. Keep them on the side until you're ready to serve—they will get soggy in the soup after a few minutes.

Kale Chips: These provide a healthy crunch and a boost of vitamins. Wash and thoroughly dry kale leaves and remove the tough stems. Toss the leaves with a bit of olive oil and your preferred seasonings, spread them out on a baking sheet, and bake them at 325°F (165°C) until they become crispy.

Pita Chips: Similar to regular croutons made of bread, but thinner and crispier. Cut pita bread into triangles, season with herbs and spices, drizzle generously with olive oil, and bake at 350°F (175°C) for 10 minutes, or until they're crispy.

The key to great crunchy toppings is to add them just before serving your soup. This helps maintain their texture and prevents them from becoming soggy in the hot liquid. Experiment with different combinations to find the perfect crunchy topping that complements your soup's flavors.

Coconut Corn Soup

This soup reflects the best of summer with sweet corn kernels, spices, and aromatics steeped in coconut milk. You can substitute frozen corn and experience the comfort of this gentle soup in colder months as well. Make sure to thoroughly brown the onion, garlic, ginger, and spices in order to access their complete flavor bandwidth before dousing them in coconut milk.

SERVES 4 TO 6

1 large onion, peeled

2 tablespoons vegetable oil

2 garlic cloves, peeled, or 1 teaspoon Garlic Paste (page 163)

2-inch (5 cm) piece fresh ginger, peeled

1 red Thai chile

1 teaspoon ground cumin

½ teaspoon ground coriander

1 tablespoon kosher salt

1 teaspoon black pepper

1 carton (32 ounces/907 g) vegetable broth

4 cups (680 g) fresh or frozen corn kernels

1 can (13.5 ounces/400 ml) full-fat coconut milk

¼ cup (60 ml) freshly squeezed lime juice

1½ teaspoons toasted sesame oil

Chopped fresh cilantro, for garnish

Dice the onion into ½-inch (1 cm) pieces. Add the onion to a large pot along with the vegetable oil and set over medium heat. Cook the onion for 4 to 5 minutes, stirring occasionally, until soft and translucent.

While the onion is cooking, thinly slice the garlic cloves, if using, and grate the ginger. Slice the Thai chile in half lengthwise and remove or keep as many seeds as you want, depending on your spice tolerance. Thinly slice the chile.

Add the garlic slices or paste, the ginger, cumin, coriander, your preferred amount of chile, and the salt and pepper to the onion. Let cook for another 5 minutes, until everything is fragrant and lightly browned.

(continued)

Add the olive oil, onion, garlic, ginger, and salt to a large pot. (You can use the same heavy-bottomed pot you used to char the peppers; just let it cool down a bit first.) Set the heat to medium-low and cook, stirring occasionally, for 3 to 4 minutes, until the garlic and ginger are lightly browned and no longer raw. Add the tahini and stir until everything is combined and the tahini begins to dry out, about 2 minutes.

Increase the heat to medium and add the charred peppers, carrots, sweet potatoes, cumin, cinnamon, turmeric, and cayenne. Stir together until the aromatics and tahini completely coat the veggies and they begin to soften, about 5 minutes.

Pour in the vegetable broth and 2 cups (480 ml) water and bring the mixture to a boil. Reduce the heat to low, cover the pot, leaving the lid slightly ajar to let steam escape, and let the soup simmer for 20 to 25 minutes, until the carrots and sweet potatoes are tender.

Remove the pot from the heat and use an immersion blender to puree the soup until smooth and creamy. Or transfer the soup to a regular blender, working in batches if necessary.

Season with black pepper to taste. Adjust the salt to your preference. Ladle the soup into bowls and garnish with cilantro.

Herby Bean and Potato Soup

Take advantage of naturally starchy ingredients in winter (or soup season, as I like to call it). Simmering potatoes and beans together releases powerful starches that create a silky smooth texture once blended. This recipe calls for reserving some potato chunks so there's some bite to the finished soup, but feel free to blend the entire pot for a velvety texture from start to finish.

SERVES 4 TO 6

1 medium onion, peeled

4 garlic cloves, peeled, or 2 teaspoons Garlic Paste (page 163)

4 medium russet potatoes, peeled

2 tablespoons olive oil

1 tablespoon kosher salt

1 teaspoon black pepper

1 teaspoon dried rosemary

1 carton (32 ounces/907 g) vegetable broth

2 cups (480 ml) unsweetened oat or soy milk

1 medium bunch fresh dill

1 can (15 ounces/425 g) cannellini beans, rinsed and drained

2 packed cups (6 ounces/170 g) packed baby spinach

Grated zest and juice of 1 lemon

Cut the onion in half. Place the cut sides down on the cutting board and cut each half into thin slices. If using garlic cloves, grate them with a Microplane and set aside. Chop 2 of the potatoes into 2-inch (5 cm) chunks. Dice the remaining 2 potatoes into 1-inch (2 cm) pieces and set aside separately.

Add the onions and olive oil to a large pot and set it over medium heat. Cook for about 5 minutes, until the onions become translucent. Add the garlic, the large potato chunks, the salt, pepper, and rosemary. Cook, stirring occasionally, for about 8 minutes, until the garlic becomes fragrant and golden brown.

Pour in the vegetable broth and milk and stir, making sure to scrape the bottom of the pot for any bits of garlic or herbs. Bring to a boil. Cover the pot, leaving the lid slightly ajar to let steam escape, and reduce the heat to low. Simmer for 10 minutes, or until the potatoes are tender when pierced with a fork or knife.

Take the soup off the heat and use an immersion blender to blend it in the pot until completely smooth and creamy. Or transfer the soup to a regular blender, working in batches if necessary, and return all the soup to the pot.

Set the pot over medium heat and add the reserved potatoes. Roughly chop half of the dill and add it to the soup. Stir in the cannellini beans and baby spinach. Simmer the soup for at least another 15 minutes, until the potatoes are tender when pierced with a fork or knife.

Turn off the heat once the potatoes are tender. Stir the lemon juice into the soup. Taste for salt and acidity and adjust to your preference. Ladle the soup into bowls and garnish with the remainder of the dill and the lemon zest.

Creamy Tomato Orzo Soup

Unlike the South's long tomato growing season, peak tomato season is limited in colder regions, so this recipe calls for tomato paste to ensure your soup is bursting with flavor, no matter what time of year you make it.

SERVE 4 TO 6

1 medium onion, peeled

4 garlic cloves, peeled, or 2 teaspoons Garlic Paste (page 163)

2 tablespoons olive oil

1 tablespoon tomato paste

1 tablespoon kosher salt

1 or 2 large sprigs fresh basil

1 carton (32 ounces/907 g) vegetable broth

2 cups (300 g) cherry tomatoes

1 cup (224 g) orzo pasta

¾ cup (180 ml) full-fat coconut milk

1 teaspoon dried oregano

½ teaspoon dried thyme

Black pepper

Chopped fresh basil or parsley leaves, for garnish

Dice the onion into ½-inch (1 cm) pieces and add to a large pot. Thinly slice the garlic cloves, if using, and set aside.

Add the olive oil to the onions and set the pot over medium heat. Cook for about 5 minutes, until they become translucent. Add the garlic, tomato paste, and salt and cook, stirring constantly for 4 to 5 minutes, until the tomato paste is deep brown.

Add the basil sprig, vegetable broth, and 1 cup (150 g) of the cherry tomatoes and bring to a boil. Stir in the orzo. Reduce the heat to low. Simmer for 10 to 12 minutes, stirring occasionally so the orzo doesn't stick to the bottom of the pot, until the orzo is al dente.

Add the coconut milk, oregano, thyme, and the remaining cherry tomatoes and stir well. Simmer for another 5 minutes to allow the tomatoes to soften. Taste the soup and season with salt and pepper.

Ladle the soup into bowls and garnish with chopped basil.

Kale Porridge with Crispy Garlic Chips

A twist on Southern-style porridge, this savory kale-based soup is ridiculously simple thanks to the power of garlic and its dual applications. Start by making the garlic chips so that the rest of the soup builds flavor onto the garlic-infused oil and softened onion base. Simmer rice in the soup base for added creaminess without heaviness.

SERVES 4 TO 6

10 garlic cloves, peeled

2 large yellow onions, peeled

1 large bunch kale, washed and dried

¼ cup (60 ml) olive oil

1 cup (224 g) Arborio rice

2 teaspoons kosher salt

1 teaspoon black pepper

1 carton (32 ounces/907 g) low-sodium vegetable broth

Slice the garlic cloves crosswise into thin chips and transfer to a large pot. Dice the onions into ½-inch (1 cm) pieces. Remove the ribs from the kale, finely chop them, and set aside. Roughly chop the kale leaves and set aside separately.

Line a large plate with paper towels and set it next to the stove. Add the olive oil to the garlic and set the pot over medium heat. Constantly stir the garlic as it fries and releases bubbles, to ensure it evenly browns, about 5 minutes. Remove the garlic chips with a slotted spoon as soon as they begin to turn golden brown and spread them out on the paper towel–lined plate. Do not wait until the garlic chips are completely golden—they will continue to cook from residual heat after you remove them.

Keep the pot of garlic-infused oil over medium heat and add the rice, onions, kale ribs, salt, and pepper. Stir continuously until the rice begins to look translucent around the edges and the onions and kale ribs have softened completely, about 8 minutes.

(continued)

Add the kale leaves, vegetable broth, and 2 cups (480 ml) water to the pot. Increase the heat to high and bring to a boil. Once vigorously boiling, reduce the heat to low. Simmer for 30 minutes, uncovered, until the mixture has thickened to a creamy soup-like consistency. Taste a grain of rice to see if it is fully cooked and soft. Once the rice is tender and cooked through, turn off the heat. Use an immersion blender to blend the soup in the pot until mostly smooth, leaving some bits of rice and kale intact. Or transfer the soup to a regular blender, working in batches if necessary.

Taste the soup for salt and pepper and adjust the seasoning to your preference. Ladle the soup into bowls and top with the garlic chips.

Sweets & Treats

The South is known for decadent cakes and pies that make up the bulk of the classic American dessert canon. Here you can choose from a sweet tea-spiked cake, an over-the-top banana pudding, a classic chocolate cream pie, and more.

Blackberry Tahini Cobbler

Consisting of just filling plus topping, the classic cobbler is perfect in its simplicity and ripe for the creation of unique flavor combinations. This cobbler employs tahini, which adds savory nuttiness while helping to bind the cobbler batter without any need for butter or eggs.

SERVES 4 TO 6

FILLING

6 cups (900 g) fresh or frozen blackberries

¼ cup (50 g) granulated sugar

2 tablespoons cornstarch

1 tablespoon freshly squeezed lemon juice

½ teaspoon kosher salt

COBBLER TOPPING

1 cup (125 g) all-purpose flour

1 loosely packed cup (220 g) brown sugar, plus more for sprinkling

¾ cup (180 ml) unsweetened oat milk

¼ cup (60 g) tahini

2 teaspoons baking powder

Plant-based vanilla ice cream, for serving

Preheat the oven to 375°F (190°C).

If using fresh blackberries, wash and dry them. Add 4 cups (600 g) of the blackberries, the sugar, cornstarch, lemon juice, and salt to a large saucepan and set over medium-high heat. Simmer and stir for 10 minutes, until the mixture begins to bubble and release steam. Turn off the heat and stir in the remaining 2 cups (300 g) blackberries. Transfer the filling to a 9 × 9-inch (23 × 23 cm) baking dish and set aside.

Add the flour, brown sugar, oat milk, tahini, and baking powder to a large mixing bowl. Fold everything together with a silicone spatula until fully combined and no streaks of flour remain. Evenly dollop the topping over the filling and sprinkle with an extra pinch of brown sugar. Bake for 30 to 35 minutes until the topping is golden brown and the filling is bubbling.

Let the cobbler cool before serving with a scoop of vanilla ice cream.

Sweet Potato and Cornflake Streusel Casserole

It is a shame that sweet potato desserts tend to get attention only during the holidays—this casserole is simple to make and delicious to eat any season. The sweet-and-salty cornflake streusel and oat milk base sets this dessert apart from classic versions of sweet potato casserole.

SERVES 9 TO 10

SWEET POTATOES

2 tablespoons (30 g) plant-based butter, plus more for greasing the baking dish

2 pounds (900 g) sweet potatoes or yams

½ cup (120 ml) unsweetened oat milk

½ cup (120 ml) maple syrup

1 teaspoon pure vanilla extract

½ teaspoon ground cinnamon

½ teaspoon ground cardamom

¼ teaspoon ground nutmeg

¼ teaspoon kosher salt

CORNFLAKE STREUSEL TOPPING

2 cups (60 g) cornflakes

4 tablespoons (60 g) plant-based butter, at room temperature

¼ cup (30 g) all-purpose flour

¼ packed cup (55 g) brown sugar

½ teaspoon kosher salt

Preheat the oven to 375°F (190°C). Lightly grease a 9 × 9-inch (23 × 23 cm) baking dish.

Peel the sweet potatoes and cut them into 1- to 2-inch (2 to 5 cm) pieces. Place the sweet potatoes in a large pot and cover them with water. Set the pot over medium-high heat and bring to a boil. Cook until the sweet potatoes are tender, 10 to 15 minutes.

Drain the sweet potatoes and transfer them to a large mixing bowl.

(continued)

Melt the butter in a small bowl in the microwave on low power for 20 seconds or in a small saucepan over low heat for 3 minutes. Add the oat milk, maple syrup, melted butter, vanilla, cinnamon, cardamom, nutmeg, and salt to the sweet potatoes. Mash and mix well until smooth and creamy. Transfer the mashed sweet potatoes to the baking dish, spreading them out evenly.

In a separate bowl, combine the cornflakes, butter, flour, brown sugar, and salt. Use your fingers to press the butter into the dry ingredients, simultaneously crushing the cornflakes. The final texture should resemble pebbly sand. Sprinkle the streusel evenly over the sweet potatoes.

Bake for 25 to 30 minutes, until the top is golden and crispy. Let cool for a few minutes before serving.

Sesame Chocolate Chip Cookies

Hundreds of years ago, sesame found its way into the heart of Southern food, and now it finds its way into chocolate chip cookies. Both sesame seeds and sesame oil boost the nutty notes and toffee flavors in the classic cookie. These cookies are perfect for making large batches, portioning into balls, and freezing for a quickie, fresh-baked cookie in a moment's notice.

MAKES 12 COOKIES

½ cup (80 g) white sesame seeds

¼ cup (40 g) black sesame seeds

1½ cups (190 g) all-purpose flour

1 teaspoon cornstarch

½ teaspoon baking soda

½ teaspoon kosher salt

1 packed cup (220 g) dark brown sugar

1 cup (2 sticks/230 to 250 g) plant-based butter, at room temperature

1 teaspoon toasted sesame oil

1 tablespoon ground flaxseed

1 teaspoon pure vanilla extract

1 cup (240 g) vegan chocolate chips, plus more for sprinkling

Preheat the oven to 375°F (190°C). Spread out the white and black sesame seeds on a baking sheet. Toast them in the oven for 5 minutes, until lightly browned on the edges. Set aside to cool. Turn off the oven.

Whisk the flour, cornstarch, baking soda, and salt together in a large mixing bowl. Add the toasted sesame seeds and whisk again to combine.

Add the brown sugar, butter, and sesame oil to another large mixing bowl or the bowl of a stand mixer. Use an electric hand mixer or the paddle attachment to beat everything together until the color has lightened and the mixture is visibly more aerated and fluffy, about 5 minutes.

In a small bowl, mix the flaxseed and 2 tablespoons water to make a flax "egg." Add the flax "egg" and vanilla to the wet ingredients and mix again until completely homogenous.

(continued)

Add the dry ingredients and chocolate chips to the wet ingredients and use a silicone spatula to fold everything together until no streaks of flour remain. Wrap the dough with plastic wrap and refrigerate for at least 30 minutes, or up to 24 hours. If you're baking the cookies more than a day after making the dough, put it in the freezer. Thaw the dough on the counter for 1 hour before baking.

When you're ready to bake, preheat the oven to 325°F (165°C). Use a cookie scoop or large spoon to portion the dough into 2-inch/⅓-cup (5 cm/85 g) balls and arrange them on a large ungreased cookie sheet at least 2 inches (5 cm) apart. Sprinkle a few extra chocolate chips on top of each cookie.

Bake for 12–15 minutes, until the center of the cookies looks just set. Use an offset spatula to gently transfer the cookies to a wire rack to cool for at least 5 minutes before serving. Let any leftover cookies cool completely before storing them in an airtight container for up to 3 days.

Note: To freeze the dough, portion it into balls and arrange them next to each other on a baking sheet. Place the baking sheet in the freezer to solidify the dough. After an hour, transfer the dough balls to a large resealable bag or airtight container and return them to the freezer for up to 3 months.

Silky Dark Chocolate Cream Pie

Silken tofu has been the star of delicate desserts for over 2,000 years in East Asia and has finally made headway into mainstream Western vegan recipes. This chocolate pie is drenched in chocolatey flavors from two directions—melted semisweet chocolate and bloomed unsweetened cocoa powder. Adding a dash of vanilla extract and espresso powder to the chocolate filling deepens the cocoa notes. Make this pie up to 3 days before you want to serve it, or even freeze it for up to 2 months. Just make sure to thaw it in the fridge overnight.

MAKES ONE 9-INCH (23 CM) PIE OR 8 SERVINGS

Tender Pie Crust (recipe follows)

2 bars (4 ounces/113 g each) vegan semisweet baking chocolate

½ cup (100 g) granulated sugar

¼ cup (20 g) unsweetened cocoa powder

¼ cup (60 g) unrefined coconut oil

1 teaspoon pure vanilla extract

1 teaspoon espresso powder

½ teaspoon kosher salt

1 package (12 ounces/340 g) soft silken tofu, chilled

Actually Whipped Cream (page 161), whipped

Preheat the oven to 350°F (175°C).

On a lightly floured work surface, roll out the pie crust to a 12-inch (30 cm) diameter circle and gently fit it into a 9-inch (23 cm) dish. Use a fork to dock the crust, making numerous holes across the base and sides. Crimp the edge with your fingers or press it onto the rim of the pie dish with the tines of the fork. Cover the pie crust with a 12 × 12-inch (30 × 30 cm) square of parchment paper and fill with pie weights or uncooked rice. Rest the pie dough in the freezer for one hour. Bake for 60 minutes with the pie weights, until the crust has set and is golden brown around the edges.

Remove the pie dish from the oven and carefully remove the parchment paper and pie weights. Return the crust to the oven and bake for another 20 minutes, or until golden brown. Set aside to cool.

(continued)

Chocolate-Bottom Pecan Pie

The bottom of this nutty, caramel-y pie is a delicious base layer of smooth, bittersweet chocolate. Instead of only pecans, adding walnuts to your regular pecan pie formula adds some textural and flavor nuance that tastes even more heavenly against the chocolate bottom. Serve with Actually Whipped Cream (page 161) for extra indulgence.

MAKES ONE 9-INCH (23 CM) PIE OR 8 SERVINGS

Tender Pie Crust (page 128)

1½ cups (180 g) pecans

1½ cups (180 g) walnuts

2 tablespoons ground flaxseed

1 cup (240 ml) light corn syrup

½ loosely packed cup (110 g) brown sugar

¼ cup (30 g) cornstarch

2 tablespoons (30 g) plant-based butter

1 teaspoon pure vanilla extract

¼ teaspoon kosher salt

½ cup (120 ml) unsweetened oat milk

½ cup (40 g) unsweetened cocoa powder

¼ cup (60 g) unrefined coconut oil

1¾ cups (420 g) vegan semisweet or dark chocolate chips

Actually Whipped Cream (page 161), whipped, for serving (optional)

Preheat the oven to 350°F (175°C).

On a lightly floured work surface, roll out the pie crust to a 12-inch (30 cm) diameter circle and gently fit it into a 9-inch (23 cm) dish. Crimp the edge with your fingers or press it onto the rim of the pie dish with the tines of a fork. Cut a 12-inch-long (30 cm) sheet of aluminum foil into strips 3 inches (8 cm) wide and 12 inches (30 cm) long. Use the strips to cover the edge of the pie crust. Set the pie crust aside to chill in the fridge.

Chop the pecans and walnuts into ½-inch (1 cm) pieces. Spread out the nuts on a baking sheet and toast in the oven for 10 minutes, until fragrant and lightly browned. Set aside to cool.

(continued)

In a small bowl, mix the flaxseed with ⅔ cup (160 ml) water. Set aside to thicken. Place the corn syrup, brown sugar, cornstarch, and butter in a medium saucepan and set over medium heat. Whisk until the sugar and cornstarch have completely dissolved, about 3 minutes. Add the flaxseed mix, vanilla, and salt and continue to whisk for another 3 minutes, or until the mixture begins to thicken and release steam. Add the nuts and remove from the heat. Set aside.

Remove the pie crust from the fridge. Combine the oat milk, cocoa powder, and coconut oil in a medium microwavable bowl and microwave for 1 minute, until the mixture releases visible steam. (If you don't have a microwave, combine the oat milk, cocoa powder, and coconut oil in a small saucepan and simmer on medium heat for 5 to 7 minutes, until it begins to release steam. Immediately remove from the heat.) Add the chocolate chips to the milk mixture and let it sit for about 2 minutes, until they begin to melt. Whisk everything together until completely smooth. Continue whisking until the mixture becomes thicker and lukewarm to the touch, about 5 minutes. Pour the chocolate base into the crust and use a silicone spatula to spread it evenly.

Return the nut filling to low heat and mix with a silicone spatula just enough to loosen it. Spread it over the chocolate layer. Keep the edges of the crust from burning by covering them with 2-inch-wide (5 cm) strips of aluminum foil. Place the pie dish on a baking sheet and bake for 45 minutes, until the top layer is slightly puffy in the center and gently jiggles when moved around.

Remove the baking sheet from the oven and carefully remove the aluminum foil from the crust to allow it to continue browning. Return the pie to the oven for another 5 to 10 minutes, until the edges of the filling are set but the center is still jiggly when you shake the baking sheet. The total bake time should be 50 to 60 minutes.

Let the pie cool completely before serving. Slice and enjoy as is or with a dollop of Actually Whipped Cream (page 161).

Peach and Mango Hand Pies

Nothing beats eating a juicy ripe peach or mango over the sink, but when you're left with a few stone fruits that aren't quite as ripe, you won't regret transforming them into a supple hand pie. A touch of grated ginger will emphasize the floral notes of whatever fruit you're using, so make sure to use a fresh knob.

MAKES 16 TO 18 HAND PIES

3 large peaches
(about 1 pound/450 g total)

2 large mangoes
(about 1 pound/500 g total)

6 tablespoons (75 g) granulated sugar

2 tablespoons cornstarch

½ teaspoon kosher salt

½ teaspoon pure vanilla extract

1-inch (2 cm) piece fresh ginger

Tender Pie Crust (page 128), or 1 package (17.3 ounces/490 g) vegan puff pastry, thawed according to package instructions

1 tablespoon unsweetened plant-based milk

1 tablespoon (15 g) plant-based butter

Set a large pot of water over high heat and bring to a boil. Once boiling, add the peaches and let them boil for 30 seconds. Use tongs or a slotted spoon to transfer them to a large bowl, and immediately place under cold running water to chill. Allow the peaches to sit in the cold water for 5 minutes. Set the pot aside.

Remove the peaches from the water and peel off the skin with a knife, or pinch it off with your fingers. (The skin should come off easily.) Cut the peaches in half, remove and discard the pits, and dice the peach flesh into 1-inch (2 cm) cubes.

Use a vegetable peeler to peel the mangoes. Slice the mangoes in half lengthwise, keeping the knife as close to the pits as possible, then cut

(continued)

down along the other side of the pits. Slice off any flesh still attached to the pits. Dice all the mango flesh into 1-inch (2 cm) cubes.

Add the peaches, mangoes, ¼ cup (50 g) of the sugar, the cornstarch, salt, and vanilla to the large pot. Use a Microplane to grate the ginger directly into the pot. (No need to peel it, as the skin will dissolve into the fruit filling.) Set the pot over medium heat and stir for about 15 minutes while the fruits release their juice and it turns into a syrup. Once the fruit syrup leaves a thick coating on the back of a spoon, remove the pot from the heat and transfer the filling to a large bowl to cool in the refrigerator for 30 minutes.

While the filling cools, prepare the crust. On a lightly floured work surface, roll out the pie crust to a 14 × 14-inch (35 × 35 cm) square. Use a pastry cutter or sharp knife to cut the dough into 4 squares across and 4 squares down, resulting in a total of 16 individual squares of dough. If using puff pastry, roll each sheet of puff pastry into a 12 × 12-inch (30 × 30 cm) square. Cut each square into 9 squares per sheet. You should end up with 18 squares. The cut squares will be about 4 × 4 inches (10 × 10 cm).

Preheat the oven to 350°F (175°C).

Line a large baking sheet with parchment paper and set it next to your workstation. Set a small bowl of room temperature water and a pastry brush next to your workstation, along with a fork. Add the milk and butter to a small bowl and microwave for 20 seconds, until the butter is mostly melted. (If you don't have a microwave, heat the milk and butter in a small saucepan over low heat until the butter melts, about 5 minutes.) Set this next to your workstation along with another pastry brush.

Place a heaping tablespoon of filling in the center of a dough or pastry square. Lightly brush water around the edges of the square. Fold one corner of the square over the filling on the diagonal to meet the opposite corner, forming a triangle. Use the fork to press down the edges of the triangle, crimping and sealing the pie shut. Place the pie on the lined baking sheet. Repeat with the rest of the filling and dough squares, arranging the pies on the baking sheet about 1 inch (2 cm) apart. Brush the tops of the pies with the butter-and-milk mixture.

(continued)

Bake the pies for 20 to 25 minutes, until the pies are completely golden brown. Let cool for 20 minutes before serving. Store leftovers in a resealable bag in the freezer for up to 2 months. To reheat, warm the hand pies in the oven at 350°F (175°C) for 5 minutes.

Note: To freeze unbaked hand pies, set the baking sheet in the freezer for 2 hours. Once frozen, transfer the hand pies to a large airtight container or resealable bag and return to the freezer for up to 3 months. Bake the pies straight from the freezer for a little longer, about 30 minutes total.

Freestyle It

> Take advantage of stone fruit season and use plums or nectarines in place of peaches and mangoes. You'll need about 2 pounds (950 g) of fruit altogether.

Sweet Tea Cake

The South's favorite summertime beverage takes the form of a loaf cake you can snack on for breakfast while sipping on . . . more sweet tea! Tea infuses beautifully into a basic cake batter, lacing each bite with the aromas of your favorite tea and a sweet citrus touch from the lemon glaze.

MAKES ONE 9 × 5-INCH (23 × 13 CM) LOAF CAKE OR 10 SERVINGS

CAKE

6 black tea bags

½ cup (100 g) granulated sugar

¼ packed cup (55 g) light brown sugar

¼ cup (60 ml) vegetable oil

1 cup (240 ml) unsweetened oat milk

2 tablespoons freshly squeezed lemon juice

1½ teaspoons baking powder

½ teaspoon baking soda

¼ teaspoon kosher salt

1 teaspoon pure vanilla extract

2 cups (250 g) all-purpose flour

LEMON GLAZE

⅔ cup (75 g) confectioners' sugar

Grated zest of 1 lemon

2 tablespoons freshly squeezed lemon juice

Preheat the oven to 350°F (175°C). Grease a 9 × 5-inch (23 × 13 cm) loaf pan and line it with parchment paper. Set aside.

Empty the contents of the tea bags into a large mixing bowl. Add the granulated sugar, brown sugar, and vegetable oil. Whisk everything together until the sugars dissolve into the oil. Add the oat milk and lemon juice and whisk again until fully combined. Add the baking powder, baking soda, salt, and vanilla and continue to whisk until they are fully incorporated. Finally, add the flour and gently stir the batter together until just combined.

Pour the batter into the prepared loaf pan and bake for 35 to 40 minutes, until the cake is bouncy to the touch and the edges of the cake appear to

(continued)

have released from the sides of the pan. Remove the cake from the oven and let it cool in the pan for at least 20 minutes. Invert the cake out onto a wire rack and let it cool completely.

Whisk together the confectioners' sugar, lemon zest, and lemon juice in a small bowl until smooth and well combined. Drizzle the lemon glaze over the top of the cooled cake before serving.

The cake can be stored in an airtight container at room temperature for up to 3 days or tightly wrapped and frozen for up to 2 months. If you're planning to freeze it, hold off on the glaze until you're ready to serve the cake.

Batsh*t Banana Cake

What would your banana bread taste like if you leaned into the fact that banana bread is simply . . . banana *cake*? It would taste batsh*t good. This recipe dresses up banana bread with chocolate to give it true dessert status. Topped with sweet shredded coconut flakes and chopped nuts, each slice of this cake tastes like decadence, as a true slice of cake should.

MAKES ONE 9-INCH (23 CM) CAKE OR 8 SERVINGS

1½ cups (190 g) all-purpose flour

½ cup (40 g) unsweetened cocoa powder

1 teaspoon baking powder

1 teaspoon baking soda

½ teaspoon kosher salt

3 ripe bananas

½ cup (100 g) granulated sugar

½ packed cup (110 g) brown sugar

½ cup (120 ml) unsweetened oat milk

½ cup (120 ml) vegetable oil

2 teaspoons distilled white vinegar

1 teaspoon pure vanilla extract

½ cup (120 g) vegan chocolate chips

½ cup (50 g) sweetened coconut flakes

½ cup (60 g) chopped walnuts or pecans

Preheat the oven to 350°F (175°C). Grease a 9-inch (23 cm) springform pan. Line the bottom of the pan with a 9-inch (23 cm) circle of parchment paper.

Whisk together the flour, cocoa powder, baking powder, baking soda, and salt in a large mixing bowl.

Peel the bananas and place in another large mixing bowl. Add the granulated sugar, brown sugar, oat milk, vegetable oil, vinegar, and vanilla. Whisk everything together until the bananas are blended through the mixture, with only some lumps remaining.

Pour the wet ingredients into the dry ingredients and stir until just combined and no streaks of flour remain. Fold in the chocolate chips until evenly distributed throughout the batter.

(continued)

Pour the batter into the prepared cake pan and smooth the top with a spatula. Sprinkle the coconut and nuts on the surface of the cake.

Bake for 30 to 35 minutes, until the center of the cake feels firm when poked and the edges of the cake have visibly released from the pan. Remove the cake from the oven and let cool in the pan for 10 minutes. Run a paring knife around the sides of the cake, unlatch the pan and remove it. Transfer the cake from the pan to a wire rack to cool for another 10 minutes.

Slice and serve the cake while it is still warm. Tightly wrap any leftover cake with plastic wrap and store at room temperature for up to 3 days, or freeze up to 3 months.

Good Bakers Make Oily Cakes

Using a good neutral oil rather than butter in your cake batter will contribute to a supremely moist and tender cake crumb. So is it luck or just sheer science that oftentimes plant-based cakes are as tasty as, if not tastier than, their dairy-filled counterparts?

To better understand how your choice of fat content affects a cake, take a microscope to the fat content's state at various temperatures. A cake's moisture level comes down to the melting qualities of its fat content. Oil enhances a cake's moisture level thanks to its ability to stay in liquid form at room temperature. Even after butter is creamed and baked into a cake, once the cake is baked and cooled, the butter in that cake will solidify at room temperature because it requires a higher temperature to remain in a liquid form. Oil is already liquid at room temperature, which means after the cake is baked and cooled, it will not solidify and dry out the cake's crumb.

Oil's higher moisture content effectively lubricates the protein and starch molecules in the flour, forming a structure that remains pleasantly tender and moist when baked and, most importantly, when stored in the fridge or at room temperature. This attribute is especially beneficial in vegan cakes, as it offsets the potential dryness that can occur when dairy and eggs are excluded from the recipe. And conveniently enough, canola and vegetable oil's neutral flavors won't overpower whatever ingredients or flavors you want to shine in your cakes.

Arguably, butter's purpose in a cake isn't solely dedicated to contributing moisture. Creaming butter and sugar in a cake recipe also improves the cake's aeration and ability to rise properly. In order to nail a plant- and oil-based cake with height and structure, the combination of an acid and baking soda will guarantee your cake rises with ease. Depending on your recipe's flavor profile, reach for a couple of teaspoons of fresh lemon juice or distilled white vinegar to activate the baking soda. Ultimately, neither flavor will be detectable in the final baked good.

Caramelized Banana Pudding

The power of cornstarch is not to be questioned. Thanks to its binding properties, you can have a quick and tasty pudding with no need for eggs. Caramelizing your bananas before adding them to the pudding evokes memories of bananas Foster, but in the form of a luscious pudding. Serve this in individual cups for an easy entertaining hack for dessert tables or in a large serving dish for potlucks.

SERVES 8 TO 10

CARAMELIZED BANANAS

4 ripe bananas

2 tablespoons (30 g) plant-based butter

2 tablespoons brown sugar

PUDDING

½ cup (100 g) granulated sugar

¼ cup (30 g) cornstarch

¼ teaspoon kosher salt

2 ½ cups (600 ml) unsweetened oat milk

1 teaspoon pure vanilla extract

ASSEMBLY

1 package (14.4 ounces/408 g) graham crackers

Actually Whipped Cream (page 161, optional)

Peel and slice the bananas into ½-inch-thick (1 cm) rounds. Melt the butter and brown sugar in a large nonstick skillet set over medium heat. Mix until the sugar mostly dissolves, about 8 minutes. Add the bananas and let them caramelize for 2 to 3 minutes on the underside before flipping them over to cook for another 2 to 3 minutes on the other side. The bananas should be golden brown on both sides. Transfer the caramelized bananas and any caramel sauce to a medium bowl and set aside.

Combine the granulated sugar, cornstarch, and salt in a small saucepan and set it over medium heat. Whisk everything to break up any lumps of cornstarch and sugar. Slowly pour in the oat milk while whisking constantly.

(continued)

The pudding will come to a gentle boil, releasing steam and small bubbles. Continue to whisk until the pudding thickens, about 10 minutes.

When the pudding feels heavy on the whisk, reduce the heat to low. Whisk in the vanilla. Scrape the bottom of the pan with the whisk to ensure that no bits of pudding are sticking to the pan and burning, then remove from the heat.

Put the graham crackers in a large resealable bag and seal it shut, making sure to release any excess air from the bag. Loosely wrap a kitchen towel around the bag, place it on the counter, and beat with a large bottle, rolling pin, or heavy can to crush the graham crackers. Remove half of the crushed graham crackers and set aside for garnish. Layer the rest of the crushed graham crackers on the bottom of a large serving dish or split evenly between individual serving bowls. Arrange the caramelized banana slices and any extra caramel on top of the cookie layer. Pour the warm pudding over the bananas, covering them completely. Let cool to room temperature, then refrigerate for at least 2 hours to set and chill.

Just before serving, you can top the pudding with whipped cream, if you like, and the remaining cookie crumbles. It will keep in the fridge, tightly wrapped, for up to 2 days.

Condiments & Sauces

Cooking can feel like art when you have all your favorite paints in front of you. These sauces and condiments add color and flavor to your meals and snacks. When you prepare yourself and your fridge with a selection of these make-ahead condiments and sauces, you can transform your meals into masterpieces.

Magic Mayo

No cashew can deliver the creaminess you get from a dollop of mayonnaise. Only silken tofu, in its supple glory, can take on the gentle tang and salty goodness of aioli or mayo. Silken tofu's curds have a conveniently high moisture content that replicates mayo's jiggly yet smooth texture. This sauce does almost everything a typical mayonnaise can do, so always keep it handy in the fridge for your next tomato toast (page 43).

MAKES 2 CUPS (480 ML)

- 1 package (16 ounces/450 g) soft silken tofu
- 1 tablespoon freshly squeezed lemon juice
- 1 tablespoon distilled white vinegar
- 1 tablespoon vegetable or canola oil
- 1 tablespoon white miso
- 1 teaspoon kosher salt
- ½ teaspoon granulated sugar

Add the tofu, lemon juice, vinegar, oil, miso, salt, and sugar to a food processor or blender. Blend on high speed until completely smooth. Use a spoon or silicone spatula to scrape down the sides and blend again to guarantee no bits of miso remain. Taste and adjust the salt and acidity to your preference.

Store in the fridge in an airtight container or tightly capped glass jar for up to 1 month.

Five-ish Ingredient Fruit Chutney

Somewhere between a pickled relish and a jam, chutneys present a simple format for you to make a customizable, sweet-and-savory condiment that will elevate any slice of toast, taco, burger, and more. Lean toward berries, stone fruit, pineapples, apples, or pears for the best result. You can slather this chutney wherever you'd normally use jam. Try it on biscuits (page 23) or tomato toast (page 43), or add it to your Thanksgiving dinner spread in place of cranberry sauce.

MAKES 2 CUPS (600 G)

1 red Thai chile

1 teaspoon cumin seeds

½ cup (120 ml) white vinegar

½ cup (100 g) granulated sugar

2 teaspoons grated fresh ginger

1 teaspoon kosher salt

2 cups (250 g) chopped pitted fruit such as stone fruit, apples, or pears; chopped peeled fresh pineapple; chopped rhubarb; whole berries; or seedless grapes

Slice the chile in half lengthwise, exposing the seeds. Remove or keep as many seeds as you want depending on your spice tolerance. Mince the chile and set aside.

Add the cumin seeds to a small dry saucepan and set it over medium heat. Toast the seeds by swirling the pan around for 2 to 3 minutes, until they are fragrant and slightly browned.

Add the vinegar, sugar, ginger, salt, chile, and fruit. Add ½ cup (120 ml) water and stir everything until sugar has dissolved and the ingredients are evenly distributed. Increase the heat to medium-high and bring the mixture to a low boil. Stir the chutney for 2 to 3 minutes as it bubbles. Reduce the heat to a simmer. Taste the chutney, adding more salt or sugar according to your taste. Simmer on low for another 20 minutes, or until the chutney has thickened to a gravy-like consistency.

Transfer the chutney to a sterile glass jar, cap tightly, and store in the fridge for up to month.

Copycat Sauce

There are few things that wouldn't taste delicious with a side of this sweet, tangy, and smoky concoction. Use it as a dipping sauce or condiment for fries, sandwiches, or anywhere you might use mustard. Inspired by Chik-fil-A's signature sauce, it tastes like honey mustard and barbecue sauce got together and had a baby.

MAKES ABOUT 1 CUP (240 ML)

½ cup (120 ml) Magic Mayo (page 151)

3 tablespoons maple syrup

2 tablespoons yellow mustard

1 tablespoon plant-based barbecue sauce (store-bought or Maple Mustard BBQ Sauce, page 162)

1 teaspoon garlic powder

1 teaspoon onion powder

½ teaspoon smoked sweet paprika

¼ teaspoon kosher salt

¼ teaspoon black pepper

Combine the mayo, maple syrup, mustard, barbecue sauce, garlic powder, onion powder, smoked sweet paprika, salt, and pepper in a medium bowl. Whisk everything together until no clumps of seasoning remain and the sauce is smooth. Taste the sauce and adjust the seasonings to your preference. You can add more mustard, maple syrup, or spices to suit your taste. Transfer to a jar or airtight container. Refrigerate for at least 30 minutes before using to allow the flavors to fully meld. Store for up to 2 weeks in the refrigerator.

Any-Green Pesto

Any leafy green will make for a versatile, pesto-like sauce. While kale and spinach are the most common contenders, feel free to experiment with mustard greens or Swiss chard. Even broccoli florets can be transformed into a pesto you'll want to coat your pasta in.

MAKES 2 CUPS (450 G)

3 loosely packed cups (9 ounces/250 g) spinach or kale leaves, tough stems or ribs removed

1 packed cup (60 g) fresh basil leaves

½ cup (60 g) walnuts, pistachios, or pecans

⅓ cup (60 g) nutritional yeast

¼ cup (60 ml) olive oil

4 garlic cloves, peeled

3 tablespoons freshly squeezed lemon juice

½ teaspoon kosher salt

Set a large pot of water over high heat. Set a colander in the sink to drain the greens after blanching.

Once the water comes to a vigorous boil, add the greens. Push the leaves down into the water and blanch for at least 30 seconds, but no longer than 1 minute. Carefully pour everything into the colander to drain, then immediately run cold water over the greens to stop the cooking. When they're cool, let them drain thoroughly, then squeeze out any remaining water.

Transfer the greens to a blender or food processor. Add the basil, nuts, nutritional yeast, olive oil, garlic, lemon juice, and salt. Blend for 1 to 2 minutes, until the pesto is paste-like and no visible pieces of nuts or garlic remain. Taste the pesto and adjust the seasoning to your preference.

Store the pesto in an airtight container or tightly capped glass jar in the refrigerator for up to 4 days or in the freezer for up to 3 months.

Very Good Gravy

The key to this gravy's umami flavor is hidden somewhere between frying down the alliums, mushrooms, and miso—all of which harmonize to deliver an unctuous, savory base. I prefer to keep the mushroom and onion bits in the gravy, but if you're looking for a silky smooth sauce, feel free to strain out the veggies before pouring it into your best gravy boat. This gravy goes well with mashed potatoes, Flaky Biscuits (page 23), or any roast vegetable.

MAKES 2 CUPS (680 G)

About 1 pound (450 g) cremini or portobello mushrooms

1 large yellow or white onion, peeled

2 tablespoons white or red miso

¼ cup (60 ml) hot water

2 tablespoons olive oil

3 garlic cloves, peeled and minced, or 1½ teaspoons Garlic Paste (page 163)

2 tablespoons all-purpose flour

2 cups (480 ml) vegetable broth

1 tablespoon soy sauce

1 teaspoon dried thyme

1 teaspoon maple syrup

Salt and pepper

Wipe the mushrooms clean with a paper towel. Chop them into ½-inch (1 cm) pieces including the stems, and set aside. Dice the onion as small as you comfortably can, preferably smaller than ½-inch (1 cm) pieces. Whisk together the miso and ¼ cup (60 ml) hot water in a small bowl to combine. (The hot water will help break down the miso into a smooth liquid that will mix into the sauce without clumping up.)

Heat the olive oil in a large skillet or saucepan over medium-high heat. Add the onions and sauté for 2 to 3 minutes, until they become translucent. Add the mushrooms and use a silicone spatula to spread them across the base of the skillet. Cook the mushrooms undisturbed for 5 minutes, or until they begin to brown. Once golden brown, add the dissolved miso and the garlic and stir for 5 minutes, until most of the water has evaporated and the garlic is fragrant and browned.

(continued)

Sprinkle the flour over the mushrooms and onions, stirring well to coat everything evenly. Cook for another minute to get rid of the raw flour taste. Slowly pour in the vegetable broth while stirring continuously to prevent lumps from forming. Bring to a simmer and cook for about 5 minutes until it thickens slightly. Add the soy sauce, dried thyme, maple syrup, and salt and pepper to taste.

Allow the gravy to cool slightly before serving. It will thicken further as it cools. To store, let the gravy cool completely, transfer it to an airtight container, and place a piece of plastic wrap directly onto the surface, making sure any exposed surface area of the gravy is in contact with the plastic. Cover with a lid and store in the fridge for up to one week.

Get Lost in the Sauce

Sauces are, quite literally, the glue that holds the components of a dish together, and can make or break how well your meal turns out. Building your sauce repertoire will elevate the overall tastiness of your home cooking and, most importantly, make your day-to-day cooking a breeze. Here are a few things to keep in mind while you level up your sauce work.

› Even though cashews will more often than not stay creamy in Silky Cashew Cream (page 158) when heated and simmered, there are ways to guarantee the cream stays set and cohesive as you add it to soups, curries, and sauces. Next time you're simmering a cashew cream–based pasta sauce, add a teaspoon of lemon juice or unseasoned rice vinegar to guarantee it stays smooth. Opposite to dairy-based creams, acids like lemon juice and vinegar actually stabilize cashew cream and prevent it from separating.

› Any green *will* actually work in pesto (page 154), even a thawed bag of frozen spinach or a nearly wilted bunch of parsley. Skip the blanching if using frozen greens, but definitely make sure to squeeze any excess water from the greens after thawing. In the mood for greens and a creamy sauce? Mix ½ cup (120 g) pesto with 1 cup (240 ml) Silky Cashew Cream (page 158) and you'll have yourself a green Alfredo-ish pasta sauce.

› The chutney on page 152 is made with five-*ish* ingredients so you can add whatever you like or omit what you don't like, depending on the fruit you have on hand and how you plan to use the chutney. If you have extra-sweet peaches, you may want to adjust the amount of sugar the recipe calls for and maybe add a variety of chiles. Maybe it's winter and you only have frozen blackberries on hand—consider using part balsamic vinegar and part distilled white vinegar to create deeper notes of caramel to contrast with the tart berries.

Silky Cashew Cream

Hats off to anyone who remembers to soak beans or nuts ahead of time, but that never seems to be me. Thankfully, boiling cashews helps soften them to the same degree as an overnight soak—a hack for primp-and-prepping them on short notice when you need a cashew cream sauce for a pot of mac and cheese (page 67 or 71).

MAKES 6 CUPS (1.4 KG)

4 cups (480 g) raw cashews

Kosher salt

1 cup (170 g) soft silken tofu

2 tablespoons neutral oil

Combine the cashews, 3 tablespoons salt, and 3 quarts (3 L) water in a large pot and set it over medium-high heat. Allow the water to come to a vigorous boil, then reduce the heat to medium-low and cover the pot, leaving the lid slightly ajar to let steam escape. Simmer the cashews for 30 to 40 minutes, until they are soft enough to gently cut through with a butter knife.

Drain the cashews. Transfer to a blender or food processor along with the tofu, oil, ½ teaspoon salt, and 2 cups (480 ml) water. If your blender is not large enough, you may need to work in two batches, in which case add only half of the ingredients to the blender at a time along with 1 cup (240 ml) water and repeat. Blend until the mixture is completely smooth and silky.

Store in the fridge in an airtight container, tightly capped glass jar, or resealable bag for up to 2 weeks, or freeze for up to 3 months. To use the frozen cashew cream, let it thaw in the refrigerator for 24 hours, then blend it with 1 tablespoon neutral oil for 2 to 3 minutes, until smooth and emulsified.

Actually Whipped Cream

This recipe is proof that cooking and baking is a science; it was inspired by the work of author Richard Makin. Instead of whipping coconut milk into a temporary fluff, this calls for emulsifying full-fat milk and coconut oil together into a makeshift heavy cream, then refrigerating it to set. Once chilled, it gets beaten into whipped cream just as if you were using traditional dairy heavy whipping cream.

**MAKES 2 CUPS (500 G) BEFORE WHIPPING,
4 CUPS (500 G) AFTER WHIPPING**

1 cup (240 ml) unsweetened full-fat oat or soy milk

1 cup (240 g) refined coconut oil

¼ cup (30 g) confectioners' sugar

½ teaspoon pure vanilla extract

Place the milk and coconut oil in a small saucepan over low heat or in a microwave-safe bowl. If using the microwave, heat it in 15-second increments, mixing between blasts, just until the mixture is warm to the touch. If using a saucepan, warm over low heat for 5 minutes, or until it is warm to the touch.

Pour the mixture into a blender and blend until it is emulsified, about 3 minutes. Pour into a lidded container, cover tightly, and place in the fridge to chill for at least 5 hours or up to 3 days.

Once the cream has chilled, transfer it to the bowl of a stand mixer fitted with a whisk attachment, or a large mixing bowl if you're using an electric hand mixer. Begin to whip the cream on low speed, allowing it to re-emulsify if needed, for 1 minute. Increase the speed to medium and whip until it begins to thicken like a runny batter. Add the sugar and vanilla at this point. Continue to whip until it thickens to soft or stiff peaks, as you prefer.

Serve the whipped cream immediately or store in the fridge in an airtight container for up to 6 hours. It may start to deflate, but can be rewhipped into stiff peaks.

Maple Mustard BBQ Sauce

To me the ideal barbecue sauce tastes as hot as it does sweet. An increased proportion of regular ole Dijon mustard in this sauce provides a deep warmth that balances the tomato-based acidity as well as the caramelized, sweet notes of maple syrup. Brush barbecue sauce on anything you'd normally pop on the grill, toss it into a bowl of Crispy Golden Tofu (page 52), or drench your BBQ Eggplant and Slaw Sandwiches (page 87) with it.

MAKES ABOUT 1 CUP (240 ML)

½ cup (110 g) canned tomato sauce

¼ cup (60 ml) pure maple syrup

3 tablespoons Dijon mustard

2 tablespoons apple cider vinegar

1 tablespoon soy sauce

1 tablespoon tomato paste

1 teaspoon smoked sweet paprika

½ teaspoon garlic powder

½ teaspoon onion powder

¼ teaspoon cayenne pepper

1 teaspoons kosher salt

½ teaspoon black pepper

In a medium saucepan, whisk together the tomato sauce, maple syrup, mustard, vinegar, soy sauce, tomato paste, smoked sweet paprika, garlic powder, onion powder, cayenne, salt, and black pepper until well combined.

Set the saucepan over medium-high heat and bring the sauce to a gentle boil. Stir in ½ cup (120 ml) water with a silicone spatula or wooden spoon. Reduce the heat to medium. Let the sauce simmer for 10 to 15 minutes, stirring occasionally to prevent it from burning or sticking to the pan, until it evenly coats the back of your spatula or spoon. Taste the sauce and adjust the sweetness, acidity, or spiciness according to your preference. Add more maple syrup for sweetness, apple cider vinegar for acidity, and mustard and cayenne pepper for heat.

Transfer the sauce to a serving bowl if using the same day. The sauce will thicken slightly as it cools. It will keep well in the refrigerator in a tightly capped jar for up to 1 week.

Garlic Paste

Blitz fresh garlic cloves and oil and store the paste in a jar for a timesaving hack for almost any recipe that calls for garlic.

MAKES 2 TO 3 CUPS (ABOUT 350 G)

8 ounces (225 g) garlic cloves, peeled

½ cup (120 ml) neutral oil, plus more for storage

Use a sharp paring knife to cut the hard root ends off the garlic cloves. Place the garlic and oil in a blender or food processor and blend until completely smooth. Scrape down the sides as necessary. Transfer the garlic paste to 8-ounce (250 ml) glass jars and pour 2 to 3 tablespoons more oil on top. (This will help the paste stay fresh longer.) Tightly seal the glass jars and store in the refrigerator for up to 1 month or in the freezer for up to 4 months.

Pickled Summer Corn

Take a longer-lasting snapshot of sweet summer corn by pickling it and storing it for later seasons. Summer corn is an ideal candidate for pickling. It remains slightly sweet as it takes on the tang and aromatics of whatever you throw into the pickling liquid. Whenever your pasta salads, rice bowls, tacos, or sandwiches need a refresh, turn to the jar of pickled corn in your fridge, or enjoy it as a punchy side dish.

MAKES 3 CUPS (400 G)

1 cup (240 ml) apple cider vinegar

¼ cup (50 g) granulated sugar

2 teaspoons kosher salt

1 teaspoon mustard seeds

½ teaspoon black peppercorns

¼ teaspoon red pepper flakes

2 cups (340 g) fresh corn kernels (from about 3 ears)

2 shallots, peeled and thinly sliced

Combine the vinegar, 1 cup water, sugar, salt, mustard seeds, peppercorns, and red pepper flakes in a small saucepan. Set it over medium heat and stir until the sugar and salt have dissolved. Bring to a gentle simmer, then remove from heat.

Combine the corn kernels and shallots in a large bowl. Pour in the hot pickling liquid, ensuring that the vegetables are completely submerged. Use a paper towel to cover the surface—this will keep the top of the corn covered with the pickling liquid. Allow the pickle to cool to room temperature.

Remove the paper towel and cover the bowl with plastic wrap, or transfer everything to a glass jar and cap tightly. Refrigerate for at least 24 hours to allow the flavors to develop; they will improve over time. Store for up to 1 month.

Pickle Like a Pro

When life gives you an abundance of fresh produce, pickle it. Pickling veggies—or even sturdy fruit—is a time-honored culinary tradition that not only preserves the harvest but also imparts delicious tangy flavors to a wide variety of produce. Whether you're a beginner or a seasoned pickling enthusiast, here are some tips and techniques to help you pickle any vegetable to perfection.

Choose fresh and seasonal vegetables: Start with the freshest vegetables you can find. Seasonal produce is ideal for pickling as it tends to be at its peak flavor and texture. Select firm, unblemished vegetables for the best results.

Wash and prepare thoroughly: Before pickling, scrub the vegetables thoroughly under running water to remove any dirt or contaminants. Trim off any discolored or damaged portions. Depending on your preference and the type of vegetable, you can leave it whole, slice it, or cut it into spears or chunks.

Consider blanching: Blanching is a technique that involves briefly immersing a vegetable in boiling water, then immediately cooling it in ice water. This step can help improve the texture and color of some vegetables before pickling, specifically green beans, carrots, and cauliflower.

Prepare the brine: While brining is critical for the perfect pickle, it's also very difficult to mess up. It typically consists of vinegar, water, salt, and sugar. The proportions of these ingredients can vary depending on your taste, but a one-to-one ratio of vinegar and water is always a safe and balanced bet. Adjust the ratios to achieve your desired flavor, depending on how sweet or salty your produce is. Consider more salt for sweeter fruits or veggies, and more sugar for naturally bitter produce, like okra or green bell peppers.

Customize with spices and herbs: To add depth and complexity to your pickles, experiment with different spices and herbs. Common additions include garlic cloves, dill sprigs, mustard seeds, coriander seeds, pink and/or black peppercorns, red pepper flakes, bay leaves, and cinnamon sticks. You can personalize your pickling brine with a combination of these ingredients to create unique flavor profiles.

Pack jars tightly: When placing the prepared vegetables into sterilized jars, pack them as tightly as possible without damaging them. This helps ensure that the pickling liquid fully surrounds and preserves the vegetables. Leave about ½-inch (1 cm) headspace at the top of the jar to allow for expansion.

Heat the brine: Before pouring the brine over the vegetables, make sure it's hot but not boiling. Pouring hot brine over the vegetables helps to create a proper seal and ensures that the pickles are fully immersed in the liquid.

Remove air bubbles: After adding the hot brine, use a nonmetallic utensil such as a plastic knife or chopstick to gently release any air bubbles trapped between the pieces of vegetable. Removing these bubbles ensures a more uniform pickle and can prevent spoilage.

Store and wait: Seal the jar and place the pickles in the fridge. Pickled onions will have absorbed enough brine to be tasty after just 2 hours. For most other produce, patience is key. Allow 24 hours for the flavors to develop.

Enjoy your pickles: Pickled vegetables can be used in a variety of ways. They make impressive additions to sandwiches, burgers, and salads. They can also serve as appetizers or condiments, adding a burst of flavor to your meals. Embrace the art of pickling and embark on a flavorful journey of preservation and creativity in your kitchen. You won't regret having a jar of bright, crunchy, and tangy bites to add to just about anything that needs some acidity.

Resources

Most ingredients in this book can be found in local grocery stores, but it's helpful to know which brands and stores you can always rely on. Find chickpea flour at a local Indian grocery store, where it will be called "besan" or "gram flour." Alternatively, you can also use chickpea flour from Bob's Red Mill, which is widely sold at Whole Foods. Plant-based chorizo sausage, or soyrizo, can also be found at Whole Foods or Trader Joe's, but most chain grocery stores also carry generic brands in their plant-based or vegetarian sections. When looking for nutritional yeast, look for brands like Bragg or Bob's Red Mill.

When looking for plant-based butter, the brand will play a role in how your butter tastes. Always prioritize brands like Mykonos when purchasing plant-based butter. Source tofu and miso from any brands you find at your local grocery store or Asian grocery—just make sure to pay attention to how many ounces are in each package so you have enough for the recipe. Lean on any oat milk brand so long as you purchase the fullest fat content, which will help maintain the richness in your cooking and baking.

Here is a list of basic ingredients to keep on hand.

Pantry

Chickpea Flour

Ground Flaxseed

Nutritional Yeast

Smoked Paprika

Refrigerator

Oat Milk

Silken Tofu

Puff Pastry

Plant-based Butter

White Miso

Acknowledgments

There is an overwhelmingly long list of people who helped me discover the magic of making. Thank you to my smiling elementary school mentor, Miss Myers, and my sarcastic freshman-year English teacher, Mrs. Kidd. You both helped me fall in love with words and the magic we can make with them. Without this discovery, I would have never practiced writing with joy.

I will always remember and be grateful to Katherine Cowles for granting me the opportunity to help others fall in love with the bounty of plants. Thank you to Judy Pray for gracefully modeling the power of editing and writing. Analucia Zepeda, I am in awe of your work and attention to detail, and thank you for combing through my manuscript with such love and care.

To my brother, Sadat Karim, and my sister-in-law, Jess Karim, thank you for rediscovering the South with me through your food adventures, farmers market trips, and personal histories. I will never forget my roots thanks to you.

Index

Mehreen Karim is a Brooklyn-based freelance recipe developer, writer, and pop-up chef. Her culinary style is best known for inspiring home cooks like herself to take risks in the kitchen, and she was recently named to the Future of Food 50 list by *Cherry Bombe* magazine. Mehreen was born and raised in the South, and her cooking often reflects her diverse food memories and the experiences that shaped her upbringing. While residing in New York, she continues to garner buzz around Southern cooking, as her Southern-inspired pop-up dinners sell out within minutes. When Mehreen isn't planning a menu for her next pop-up, she's writing articles or recipes for food media outlets like *Bon Appétit*, Food52, Eater, and more. Find her @reeniekarim.